ISLAND O

Other books by Connery Chappell

FICTION

Swinging Apple
Two Pleasures for your Choosing
The Arrival of Master Jinks
Trouble on the Line

NON-FICTION

Island Lifeline
The Dumbell Affair

Island of Barbed Wire

*Internment on the Isle of Man
in World War Two*

CONNERY CHAPPELL

**Foreword by
Sir Charles Kerruish** KBE, OBE

ROBERT HALE

First published in 1984

Paperback edition published in 2005 by
Robert Hale, an imprint of The Crowood Press Ltd,
Ramsbury, Marlborough, Wiltshire SN8 2HR

www.crowood.com

www.halebooks.com

This impression 2017

British Library Cataloguing-in-Publication Data
A catalogue record for this book is available from the
British Library.

ISBN 978 0 7090 7754 1

Printed and bound in India by Replika Press Pvt Ltd

Contents

List of Illustrations

Illustrations are reproduced by courtesy of the following: 3, 5, 12B, Hilary Guard Collection; 4, 13B, 14, 15, Stanley Basnett; 6–9, coupon money photos, 6, by Edward J. Kelly from the Leslie Morgan Collection; 10, Department of Fine Art, University of Newcastle.

Foreword by Sir Charles Kerruish, KBE, OBE
Former Speaker of the House of Keys

From the dawn of history the Isle of Man has been subject to the arrival of visitors—some of these visits have been unwelcome, as were the invasions of marauding Norsemen in the ninth and tenth centuries. More recently the Isle of Man has made a virtue of necessity by seeking, not unsuccessfully, to attract to its shores visitors of another sort, holiday-makers.

This book chronicles a remarkable visitation—the alien internees, and later the political detainees who, although not in arms, were regarded as threats to the security of a country engaged in a war for survival. Some of these arrivals were hostile but more were confused, puzzled, and many resentful of the fact that they were regarded as being potentially dangerous by a country they felt was home and whose cause they espoused.

They came to an island which, although only a hundred miles from places which felt the full fury of Hitler's onslaught, was remarkably insulated against the trauma of war. It was an island whose population had for the second time responded to the call to defend the free world, sending a higher percentage of its young men and women to the war than any other part of the British Islands. It was an island which was temporary home for up to 10,000 servicemen at any one time throughout the hostilities, an island which shared the concern of its neighbour across the water over the future, and the ultimate result of the war.

Connery Chappell treats this fascinating period of the Isle of

Man's history with great sensitivity. He portrays the pathos of families separated by the winds of war, human frailty, natural suspicion on the part of a population at war, the frustration of individuals at bureaucratic delays and, above all, the response of the internees which resulted in some cases in despair, in some cases in anger, in many cases in boredom, but in so many cases in the profitable use of time for self-improvement. When one considers the variety of their origin and background it is perhaps not surprising that so many men of ability passed through the Isle of Man. They were to use that time of enforced experience to exchange ideas, increase their knowledge and better equip themselves to contribute to the society to which they would ultimately return, and in many cases to achieve great eminence in their respective fields.

This book helps Manx people, the men and women who found the Isle of Man as a temporary home, and all students of the human condition to understand more fully this phase of Island history.

Acknowledgements and Sources

Much has been lost of the great mass of paperwork that a World War must have left behind in the Isle of Man. Demolition and rebuilding saw the shredding or disposal of many files, and Manx lore insists that much of the island's modern social history lies at the bottom of a disused mine working, where local officialdom tended years ago to dump its papers. Since then order has been restored.

However, the archives in the library of the Manx Museum, and to a lesser extent in the attics of Douglas, still make possible a reconstruction of life on the island as it was affected by the internment camps that mushroomed up in 1940; to do this the writer has been given access to old papers of a general nature for which he is indebted to Peter Hulme, the Manx Government Secretary, and to Frank Weedon, Chief Constable. Thanks are also due to A. Marshall Cubbon, Director of the Manx Museum, and to invaluable help from Ann Harrison, Archivist and Librarian of the Museum Library.

Alan Killip, now Superintendent and Deputy Chief Constable was a police cadet at the time and gave the writer valuable help, as did R. L. Lamming FRCS and Dr Alexander McPherson; Major Edward Brownsdon, and Sydney Shimmin, respectively Life President and Managing Director of the Isle of Man Steam Packet, who enabled a search to be made of the line's sailing-sheets; Barnet Fingerhut, who helped compile details of the

Jewish internees who died on the island during the war; Rev.
Denis Baggaley; J. A. Bregazzi; Mrs Millicent Faragher; Harvey
Briggs; M. Moore and Mrs K. McNeil, among others.

Executives of specialized organizations who dealt with
wartime internment and who contributed advice or gave material
that was used in compiling the book, included David Massel,
Executive Director of The Board of Deputies of British Jews; Dr
Werner Rosenstock, Association of Jewish Refugees in Great
Britain; Joan Stiebel, Jewish Refugees Committee; Miss M. N.
Slade, Archivist, British Red Cross Society; Major E. R. Elliott,
Corps Secretary, The Royal Pioneer Corps; J.-J. Indermühle,
Cultural Counsellor, Swiss Embassy, London; Library of the
Religious Society of Friends, London; Library of the Ministry of
Agriculture, Fisheries and Food, London; and Library of the
Ministry of Defence, London.

Local people on the Isle of Man to whom thanks are due
include Mrs E. W. H. Kellett; R. J. Kermeen; the late Alec Clague;
Mrs Joan Herring; Walter Kennedy; Mrs E. McGhee; Ken Powell;
W. E. Curphey; Leonard Fletcher; D. F. Goodyear; A. Fehle; R. D.
Quine; Maurice and Mrs Scales; Egerton Cregeen and the late
Mrs Cregeen; Albert Lowe; W. E. Cowley; E. Corteen; and J. G.
Bell.

Italians who either had direct personal knowledge of the
internment camps themselves or helped in tracing men who had
been on the island include Rev. Roberto Russo of St Peter's Italian
Church, London; Caval. P. Pini; A. Cavalli; L. Demascio; Pietro
Zinelli; Giuseppe Servini; and, of course, G. Maneta. Mrs J.
Encke of Heidelberg was also helpful, as was Dr Hermann Scholz
of Berlin.

Dr John Milner, of the Department of Fine Art, University of
Newcastle upon Tyne, gave details of the portrait painted by Karl
Schwitters of his fellow artist Fred Uhlman during their internment in Hutchinson Camp, and sanctioned its reproduction. Mr
Uhlman gave permission for an extract from his book *The Making
of an Englishman*. Alick J. Leggat, the art collector, researched the
records of the German artists interned in Onchan Camp, and
Gracia Cullen helped to trace the careers of a number of
musicians interned on the island. Specialized information on
camp 'money' was supplied by Hilary Guard and E. Quarmby.

A number of books have been written on the general subject of
the internment of aliens during the Second World War. The first

of them was *The Internment of Aliens* by F. Lafitte, published by Penguin back in 1940/41. Two others on the subject are *Collar the Lot* by Peter and Leni Gillman (Quartet Books) and *A Bespattered Page* by Ronald Stent (Deutsch). These deal with the political and ethical aspects of internment as a whole. Mr Stent, an academic who was interned in Hutchinson Camp and was then released to join the Pioneer Corps, ended the war as a Major on the General Staff at Delhi. A detailed profile of Peter Schidlof, the instrumentalist, written by Margaret Campbell, appeared in *The Strad* magazine of August 1983.

A book written after his retirement by B. E. Sargeaunt, *The Military History of the Isle of Man* (Buncle, Arbroath, 1947), deals with the Knockaloe Camp on the island in the First World War, with the internment camps of 1940 and with the Manx military effort generally.

The Manx are ardent newspaper-readers and have remained so for the best part of two centuries. The newspaper, printed, photographic and manuscript collections in the Museum at Douglas go back to the *Manx Mercury* in 1798. A century later, a small island with a population of little more than 40,000 at the time, was producing seven local newspapers, one of which was for some years a daily. At the start of World War II the local newspapers included the *Mona's Herald*, the *Isle of Man Times*, the *Isle of Man Examiner*, the *Ramsey Courier* and the *Peel City Guardian*, all of which are in the Museum archives, the *Mona's Herald* being on microfilm.

A less detailed and more recent collection of Manx source material is in the Tynwald Library, in the Government Buildings, in Douglas. This deals primarily with Manx Government publications. Collections of Manx official Standing Orders are to be found in full in the Museum and Tynwald Libraries.

Two major acknowledgements remain. The first is to Arthur Hawkey, for years Lobby Correspondent of the *London Standard*, who gave up much time for nothing more than friendship, checking dates and facts and supplying useful background material.

Lastly, the writer records the great help of his wife Joan, who played a major part in a research lasting some months and who took tireless notes of literally dozens of interviews. Without her the book would not and could not have been written.

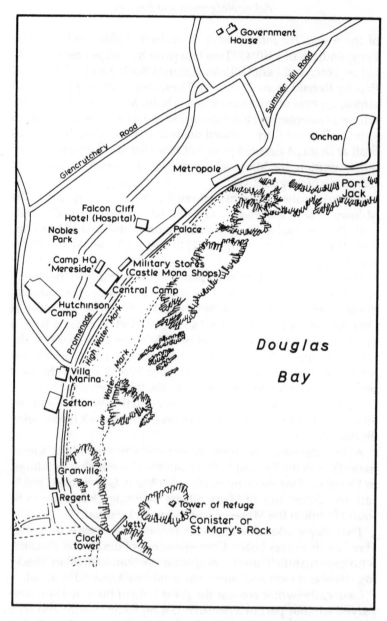

Douglas was the centre of the internment camps on the Isle of Man, and of them only the Hutchinson Camp was away from the sea front. The large Onchan Camp was just outside the town boundary.

Sketch map by P. D. Lloyd-Davies

1

Business as Usual

Wars, rumours of wars, and the ferocious run-up to war—all this was the currency of 1939, an evil year if ever there was one. Thousands were fleeing west from central Europe in terror of the concentration camps; whole countries were being bullied and seized. But the more distant the scene, the less the impact. Men were not callous; they simply led their own lives.

Thus it was in the Isle of Man, secure in the centre of the Irish Sea, less than four hours by boat from Liverpool. The Manx went about their business in their usual manner; they lived by the harvest, from the land, from the sea and from the holiday visitors. The island was a world of its own, shielded by the sea from the strut and menace of the war-merchants who stomped in Europe. It was largely poor, but it was also a place of peace; its people wanted nothing more than to live in good fellowship with their neighbours, to follow the shoals and to make what use they could of the grass that grew so lushly. The spring passed placidly, the islanders greeting the early holiday-makers and preparing for the annual invasion of motor-cycle enthusiasts for the TT races which carried the island's name round the world.

These races had changed in recent years. No longer were the machines and riders exclusively British. The French, the Germans and the Italians were designing new bikes and providing new men to ride them. A blond German named Meier had even won the Senior TT, and as the time of the early summer important races approached, the German challenge was seen to be stronger than ever. Splendid; the more competition, the more the interest in the races, and the more visitors.

Then a strange thing happened. A Manx newspaper criticized the fact that some British riders were now using foreign machines. The practice, it said, was deplorable. The writer even argued that German and Italian cycles should be barred. It was a sign, perhaps the first, that the island, although wrapped up in its own affairs, was becoming increasingly aware of the swastika strutting in Europe. A human migration was moving westwards from central Europe, but it passed by or stopped short of the small island in the Irish Sea. It is doubtful if more than a dozen of all the victims of Nazi oppression ever sought sanctuary in the Isle of Man. The great mass of refugees went on to the United States or stopped at mainland Britain.

The remarks in the *Isle of Man Times* were snubbed by no less a man than the Lieutenant-Governor, Lord Granville, the King's personal representative on the island and the embodiment of its complex relationship with the United Kingdom, which had final authority over much of its affairs; for Man was as British as Manchester, but it had a measure of self-government. At a reception after the races His Excellency repudiated the newspaper's remarks. Politics, it was obvious, must have nothing to do with sport.

The German visitors seemed pleased; they left the island after the races, promising to be back. Several of them eventually kept the promise.

The Manx removed the protective straw bales dotted along the thirty-seven miles of the racing road circuit and welcomed the holiday-makers as they came ashore in ever-increasing numbers. It was a splendid season; they were well content. Then the island authorities suddenly issued the first pamphlets from distant London about Air Raid Precautions, which were at first called War Emergency Precautions. The seaside landladies read them, a little puzzled. War? Surely not. And certainly not during the holidays.

A few weeks later the Manx government gave the official view: air attack on the island was extremely improbable. Meanwhile, the heads of the Steam Packet Company in Douglas laid the invasion plans of peace and organized forty-five crossings between the mainland and the island for the August bank holiday period. So great was the influx of visitors that the shipping line moved 70,000 people back home over the week-end of 11 August, their energy doubtless restored for whatever lay ahead. Yet as the days ticked by in August, the landladies noticed that, while the exodus was in full flood, the forward bookings for late holidays into September were hanging fire. Cancellations soon started coming in.

Nevertheless, the Manx Grand Prix, the second of the island's annual motor-cycle racing festivals, promised well. It was due to be held from 12 to 14 September and would bring down the curtain on the season; 108 entries had been received, four more than in 1938.

Then came profound shocks near the end of August. The Manx anti-aircraft territorials were called up. The Steam Packet Company was put on alert; in the ultimate emergency a number of its ships would be needed at once by the Admiralty, and men with them. It was soon realized that, if the threat to Poland developed into a full European war and if it lasted into the following year, the effect on the island could be catastrophic. The holiday trade would vanish, just as it had in the 1914 war. Suddenly the landladies were really alarmed.

'The Fuehrer knows exactly where he stands', snapped the *Manx Examiner* in its issue of 25 August. Wars and the menace of wars; the Germans had better remember that the British in general and the Manx in particular would stand for no nonsense.

A week later the *Examiner* had the island 'preparing for the worst', while announcing bravely that complete preparations had been made. That was on 1 September. On the coming Monday, 4 September, the Grand Prix practice sessions would commence, and readers were assured that the international situation would have no effect on the racing.

That week-end the threat became a reality. The full war had arrived. The Grand Prix was forgotten. It was never held. The Manx landladies filled up forms eagerly as the authorities sent out circulars asking boarding-house keepers to accept child evacuees from the mainland. It was said that nearly 15,000 were expected. They never came.

For a few days transport from the island was erratic and uncertain. Steamer services were drastically cut down, to be restored on a modified but regular basis later. Air services were cut for some months.

As on the mainland, paperwork increased rapidly: there were forms for the fishermen who were allowed a restricted inshore business; forms for the farmers; forms in abundance for the landladies, who met to discuss plans for the reception of child evacuees. Orders and directions appeared everywhere. Suddenly, it was rule by paper.

Within days landing-permits became compulsory for passengers on the Manx boats at the Liverpool landing-stage; but while it was fairly simple to get off the island, it was sheer misery to get back to it or come to it afresh. More than any other of the emergency restrictions, the Manx bitterly resented the business of passports and permit cards between Liverpool and Douglas.

It took little more than a month and a lot of shouted fury for the citizens to win the paper battle; by 6 October the need for travel documents was abolished. It had taken editorial shouts of 'Hitlerism' to do it.

Meanwhile, the landladies remained concerned for their immediate future, especially as there was no sign of those promised child evacuees. The outlook was bleak, and sensible people decided to drum up business. A meeting of the Boarding House and Apartment Association was held in Douglas in the first month of war, and a small advertisement was drawn up for the London newspapers.

ISLE OF MAN
A Really Permanent Place of Security
Safe accommodation to suit all pockets. Very
reasonable terms. Home Farm produce.
Regular mail boat services to and from Liverpool.
Write to: etc.

There was a response of sorts. But it was little more than minimal. Maybe those who wanted to escape to the country from the danger of town shied at the prospect of a sea journey on the way. So the landladies were entitled to be anxious.

After the first flurry of excitement at the shrill declaration of hostilities, many people on the island seemed to be carrying on as though nothing much had happened. War was far away, except to the family where the man had been called up to the forces. Even the arrival through the post of the first ration books caused scant comment. More than anything this was a farming

community, and it seemed only puzzling when the announce-
ments of shortages came out one by one; bacon and butter were to
be rationed, starting in the first week of the New Year. Bacon,
perhaps; but to the Manx the rationing of butter seemed almost
absurd. Cattle lived on grass, and the island would not be short of
it.

In January 1940 Sir John Anderson, then Home Secretary,
stated that there was no place in the British Isles sufficiently
removed from areas of military importance for it to be suitable to
take over a large influx of enemy aliens for internment.

Here at last was something to chew on. The Manx Chamber of
Trade soon reminded authority that the island had such advan-
tages. It had housed the main enemy alien camp in the 1914–18
War; Knockaloe became a small town holding 23,000 men, built
hut by hut near Peel on the island's west coast.

Decisions were slowly taken in London. This time there would
be no wooden huts. Many of those worried seaside landladies
were to find their problems solved, in a way they could not have
anticipated.

2

Internment by Stages

Much happened on the British mainland before the barbed wire ringed the first Manx camp, and much of it caused bitter and sustained criticism. This book confines itself to examining the life in the camps and what the internees meant to the Isle of Man; it tries not to debate the political or moral issues involved in the fact of internment itself.

However, certain facts are basic and should be given as objectively as possible. There were approximately 75,000 people of Germanic origin in Britain at the outbreak of war. Roughly 60,000 of them were refugees from Hitler, mostly Jews from Germany and Austria, the majority of whom had fled to Britain in 1939, when British authority had shown something of its old liberality towards refugees. Calculated anti-Semitism by the Nazis had risen to a shocking climax in November 1938. Men read the news sadly as the now stateless members of an ancient civilization swarmed west to escape destruction; consciences which had been conveniently silenced for some years were suddenly reasserted.

Years earlier the War Office in London had worked out a plan to take care of enemy aliens in the event of a war. It grouped them into categories, A and B. The first was for officers and gentlemen, men of position, who could afford to pay what amounted to modest mess bills, while the second was for other ranks. It was a naïve approach, and it was quite hopeless for dealing with whole hordes of refugees. It was overwhelmed. A yardstick was needed to apply to thousands.

After war broke out, it was decided that all Germans and Austrians, male or female, should appear before local Enemy Alien Tribunals and be classified into three categories: A would be doubtful risks posing potential security threat, to be interned at once. B category was where loyalty was suspect, but these could yet remain at liberty, subject to various restrictions. The C category would be for those who posed no risk and satisfied the tribunal.

Grading this mass of aliens was a rough and ready business at first. The tribunals were set up geographically, without enough regard being taken of the local population. This could result in curious imbalances; one tribunal might have to study hundreds and even thousands of cases, while another had only a few score. This meant that classification was more thorough in some places than in others; it could mean, too, that a man who would have been classified A, say, in Edinburgh, could have been classed as C, say, in Exeter. The system was later improved; the country was divided into twelve defence zones, each with an Alien Advisory Committee. But the urgency was great and the pressure from Whitehall increased as the War developed. However careful the arrangements, it was impossible to guarantee the uniformity of the grading throughout the country.

By the end of February 1940 roughly 73,000 cases were examined. It was a very imperfect and temporary end to a vast task. The result: 569 A risks, 6,782 B and about 66,000 C, where no security was involved. Rather more than 55,000 of the Cs were registered as 'refugees from Nazi oppression' and of them nine in ten were Jewish.

Such was the first stage of the internment problem. It had not proceeded without strong criticism; in a democracy nothing in the crisis of war ever does. There were complaints that within a few hours of war some of the comparatively few who had been collected for immediate internment included Jews who were violently anti-Nazi and who found themselves physically threat-ened when mixed with an intake of German merchant seamen who were violently anti-Jewish. The pattern was to be repeated all too often.

The early days, however, were relatively orderly. The chaos of mass internment was to come with the sweeping Nazi invasion of the Low Countries in the spring of 1940, when the direct threat to Britain became acute and it was decided that all male Germans between sixteen and sixty were to be interned at once. These internments began on 15 May. The administrative machinery to control them was primitive. So heavy had been the influx of refugees, it had been impossible to prepare for the numbers involved, and above all else the nation had the crisis of survival on its mind. Confusion then increased.

On 11 June 1940 the large colonies of Italians in Britain changed instantly from alien to enemy aliens. The administrative chaos was immediate. Whereas most of the Nazi refugees had not been in Britain more than a few months or at best a year or two, the Italians had usually been there for some years and were very much part of the British scene, many of them talking English and thinking British.

With the Italian entry into the war, Winston Churchill instructed the Home Secretary, Sir John Anderson, to intern all adult male Italians immediately. Desperate measures were now demanded in a dire national emergency.

Two days later the Home Secretary was able to tell the House that 10,869 had so far been interned and that this figure included all men and women in the B category.

After another week the Chiefs of Staff were calling for even more urgency. By now 12,000 had been interned from 76,000 male and female Germans and only 4,500 Italians out of 15,000. This would not do. It was simply not enough. The Home Policy Committee of the Cabinet thereupon decided to order immediate internment of all male enemy aliens between sixteen and sixty.

The wholesale rounding-up started on 25 June. Invalids, the very young and the over-60s were exempted, but so over-burdened was the machine that error after error was made; schoolboys and the seriously sick were too often picked up and interned. Men were taken from their background without warning. The allegation of callousness was levelled time and time again. The attitude of the police varied, according to the local interpretation of the rules laid down and to the facilities available.

The general order to take into internment had to be acted on, but the instructions were frequently carried out in a haphazard way and it was said that in one camp more than a third of the inmates were unfit.

A typical case among hundreds was Dr Hermann Scholz, who lived in a small flat in Westminster near the Cathedral. It was convenient for the large London hospital where he seemed to be spending most of his life. Hermann Scholz was a houseman at a leading central London hospital. He was German, young, strongly anti-Nazi and tired, as was normal with housemen, who expected to be forever overworked. He had qualified in his native Berlin and had put himself in danger from the young army of brown-shirted hysterics for speaking up against the rising Hitler.

A medical professor at Cambridge had heard of him and his troubles and invited him to Britain. He came over in the mid-1930s and continued his studies. The way to specialization was through a junior post at one of the many teaching hospitals, most of them in London. Like dozens, if not hundreds, of German and Austrian doctors who preferred British tolerance to Nazi thuggery he stepped down to plant his feet firmly on the bottom rung of the medical ladder. He settled in London and worked the long, long hours of the junior hospital doctor.

The young Dr Scholz had many German-speaking colleagues, for the escape from the Nazis had gained in pace throughout the year. But unlike most of them he was not Jewish. He was that man whom Hitler himself saluted, an Aryan; German through and through, and proud of it. He abominated Hitler, convinced the man was a sickness that would pass, but he had nothing but admiration for his native land.

When the war came, he went before a tribunal and was promptly graded as a C-category alien. His record was clear and good: he had settled down in Britain; he had guarantors of eminence in the medical faculty, and his work at the hospital made him a valuable member of the community. The mere idea of internment was ridiculous.

Had he been engaged on any sort of war work, the doctor would have stopped immediately. He disapproved vehemently of Hitler and everything about the Nazis, but Germany was Germany; he would do nothing to help her enemies. Healing the sick, however, was different. He could carry on with a clear conscience.

Hermann Scholz carried on. But not for long.

At six o'clock one June morning there was a knock on his door and he found himself being sent to Rochester Row police station by a Scotland Yard detective. At the station he found a bewildered desk sergeant, whom he knew, and a small crowd of even more bewildered Italians who jabbered nervously and ceaselessly. He had with him a case holding the shaving kit and the toothbrush he had been advised to pack, and nothing else. He then found himself being herded into a police van, of the type used for delivering prisoners to court for the hearing of their cases, known affectionately to Londoners as a Black Maria. This took them to the Oratory School in the Brompton area of west London, where an interrogation unit had been set up.

Scholz was able to explain himself. He was a German; he would do nothing against Germany. He abominated the Nazis, but he was still a German. War work? He could do nothing against Germany. The attitude was clear-cut. It is reasonably certain to have earned the young doctor a new rating.

From Brompton he went on to Kempton Park, whose race-course buildings had been converted into a transit camp for enemy aliens. In the early days the word 'transit' was theoretical; it was known for them to stay at Kempton for many weeks.

Not so the doctor. After a few days he was moved on, to Huyton, the large camp near Liverpool, converted from a half-built housing estate.

Hermann Scholz had started the journey to the Isle of Man.

The effect of internment on the Italians was one mainly of fright-ened bewilderment. So many of them had been born and brought up in Britain. Hundreds of them worked in the catering trade, while others were in industry in cities like London and Glasgow. Many spoke English with strong Scottish and northern accents. Wherever there was a job to be done and not much in the way of wages to pay for it, the Italians had been there for years, grateful for a chance to make a living.

With the Jews of Germanic, Polish and Central European extraction, the position was much more complex. They had flooded westwards in a great wave in the months before the outbreak of war, their numbers making uniform classification almost impossible in the circumstances. But they were only part of the Germanic/Jewish population of the country. Many had fled to Britain right from the start of the rise of the Nazi party. The Reichstag fire lit up the writing on the wall. Unlike the refugees who came in the desperation of 1939, many of them had had time to establish themselves as men of position, valuable to the country as a whole. They were doctors, surgeons, writers and art-dealers, publishers and theatrical producers, musicians and scientists. Some were already middle-aged and leaders in their professions; some grew old in the security of Britain. But mostly they were on the young side, doctors taking up appointments in London to train for additional medical degrees; teachers, musicians continuing their studies. Many did not even change their nationality from the country of their birth which under the Nazis was now disowning them. Many thought of themselves as belonging to no particular country, proud of their profession or calling, proud of being Jewish.

At first few people argued about the policy to intern the aliens. It was even said that the move was for their own safety as much as for national security. The majority of newspaper readers accepted that the risk of a Fifth Column in Britain could spring from the freedom of thousands of enemy aliens who might include Nazi agents and saboteurs. The popular Press was not on the side of the aliens. They were an easy target. It made good copy.

The SS *Marzocco* was homeward bound from Newcastle upon Tyne carrying a cargo of 9,000 tons of coal. She was registered in Genoa, where she was bound, and her life was spent normally in the coal trade between Italy and the Baltic ports. All that had changed. The Nazi obliteration of Poland had abruptly stopped such traffic, the British now blockaded the entrances to the Baltic, and the Italian colliers now traded in British ports and bought British coal.

It was not an easy trade. The British Navy had established shipping lanes that had to be followed by all or disobeyed at peril. Yet the Western Front had collapsed and the British Army had escaped back home in disorder. Britain faced inevitable surrender in a few weeks. The French were routed and soon Il Duce would lead a victorious Italy into a short mopping-up war alongside the invincible Germans. So thought Captain Giuseppe Marini of the

Marzocco as he left Newcastle on the tide, a British pilot aboard just as in normal peacetime. Other ships could be seen astern as he steamed northwards from the river to the North Sea.

Down below Giovanni Moneta sat in the crew's recreation room, reading an old Italian newspaper. He spoke barely a word of English and he was far behind on the world news. The crew's radio, which was not the best of sets even when they were in home waters and reception was easy, was busy with Neapolitan songs, which came through fitfully, interspersed with Morse and static.

Moneta was a ship's engineer, a young man of rising twenty-five. His family came from Milan in the north of Italy, but he had been brought up on the island of Elba, where he had lived until he joined the merchant navy. He was quiet, a good worker, and he knew his engines. Had he gone through university, he would by now have been a ship's officer, but such was the Italian system that as a working engineer further promotion was barred him.

Suddenly he heard the news on the radio.

The waiting was over. The Duce had said the word. Italy was now at war. They had left Newcastle while to them it was still a neutral port. Now, quite simply, it was an enemy.

Moneta dropped the old newspapers and ran up to the bridge. Captain Marini took the news calmly. In any case he had been expecting it daily. He realized at once that a Fascist ship's captain could not continue sailing under enemy pilotage. There were on board thirty people, a British pilot and a ship's company of twenty-nine. There were two lifeboats. The pilot was given one and they cast him off.

They continued northwards, all twenty-nine of them, the minefields to starboard. The captain knew that it was only a matter of time. Aberdeen was below the horizon astern to port when a British aircraft sighted them and it became necessary for him to give his final orders. Moneta went below and smashed the ship's condensers. She was heavy in the water, and her engine-room started flooding almost at once. There were explosions as great billows of steam and water burst amidships.

The crew took to the remaining lifeboat in orderly fashion. The SS *Marzocco* was never to fall into the hands of the British. She broke in two and went down quickly.

The crew beached on Salt House Mead in one party.

Within the hour twenty-nine Italians were inside the forbidding pink granite of Peterhead's convict prison, built by its inmates in the grim 1880s.

They had started on the long tack to the Isle of Man.

The crew of the SS *Marzocco* did not stay in Peterhead more than a week. They were taken by coach to Edinburgh, were interned in the castle and were behind barbed wire for the first time. The wire was a commodity that had not been needed in the convict prison on the headland in the far north. They were together as a party and so were to remain for a long, long time.

Edinburgh's historic castle housed them for three weeks. They were not in cells or any sort of solitary confinement but were kept together in one large room, which suited them. Moneta makes no criticism of the British officers who, he says, had had no opportunity to get things properly organized. The only remembered complaint is that the toilets were inaccessible at night, and the only convenience was a dustbin placed for the night in the centre of the room where the party lived.

At the end of three weeks the Italian seamen were transferred. In common with all the other internees temporarily held in the castle, they were medically examined and questioned as to their birthplace, their work and so on; in their case the interviews were short and to the point. They were enemy merchant seamen, young and suitable for maritime service to the Italian Navy. As such they very decidedly came into the A internment category. Theirs was likely to be a long war.

The only doubt was whether they should be sent to the Isle of Man or trans-shipped to Canada.

They were lucky. Landing at Douglas, they were marched off to the Metropole Camp, Captain Marini at their head.

The disorganization in the control of internment was at its worst following the massive collections of B- and C-class internees in June 1940, and it remained so during July.

Nowhere was it more chaotic than in the transport of some thousands to the Dominions, which had agreed to take very limited numbers.

In all, approximately 11,400 Germans and Italians were sent

to Canada or Australia, more than 400 of them setting sail twice, as they were torpedoed on their first trip, brought back to Britain and then sent off a second time. Five ships were involved, four sent to Canada, of which one was lost, and one to Australia.

First of them was the *Duchess of York*, which sailed on 21 June, with a complement of 2,100 A-class German internees which included approximately 1,700 merchant seamen and 500 prisoners of war.

The second sailing was the *Arandora Star*, which left Liverpool in the early hours of 1 July with roughly 480 A-class Germans and merchant seamen and 730 Italians of seemingly mixed and doubtful classifications; official figures differed. The ship was sunk the next day. Of the total complement of 1,200 only 530 were saved.

Two other ships took aliens to Canada, the *Ettrick*, which took 1,300 B- and C-class Germans and approximately 1,350 German prisoners of war, and the *Sobieski*, with 400 Italians, nearly 1,000 B and C Germans and 450 German POWs.

Only one ship went to Australia, the troopship *Dunera*, carrying nearly 2,300 B- and C-class Germans, 200 Italians and nearly 250 A-class Germans.

Conditions varied; in at least one ship they were disgraceful. The voyage of the *Dunera* was a sad page in modern shipping history. Built to take 2,000 men, she carried a total of nearly 2,900 including crew and escort. The precise figures have been argued but it has been accepted that 1,150 were B and C German internees from Huyton, 830 from the Isle of Man and 300 from Lingfield. There were also approximately 440 survivors from the *Arandora Star*, consisting of 200 Italians and 240 German A-class which included some seamen.

The voyage took eight long weeks. Australian officials meeting the ship at Fremantle were said to have been deeply shocked at the living-conditions the internees had endured. Ill-treatment had varied from beatings to robbery with violence. Cases of belongings had been claimed as the men boarded the ship, were piled up on deck and ransacked during the next few weeks. Personal possessions such as rings, fountain pens and wrist watches were snatched by the ill-disciplined escort. Even safety razors were confiscated. The internees mostly lived in largely unfurnished holds in the depths of the ship where the heat and the stench were very bad. They had only brief periods on deck, guarded by troops with fixed bayonets. The food was poor, and for days on end the seasickness in such conditions added to the utter squalor.

News of the conditions aboard took a long time getting back to Britain, but slowly the letters came through from the internees in their new land. Protests were immediate but action was slow. Eventually there were inquiries, and the Government decided to give the internees compensation for their losses. There were also three court martials, starting on 20 May 1941, one of which resulted in an RSM getting a year's imprisonment and being dismissed the service.

To the larger British public the voyage of the *Dunera* was at best an item in the small print. The loss of the *Arandora Star* became public almost at once and caused a sensation.

She was a famous luxury cruise liner, pressed into war service, still not fitted out as a troop carrier and not suitable for large consignments of internees. So her complement was only 1,200 and the conditions were nothing like as horrific as those on the *Dunera* proved to be when she set off nearly a fortnight later. What was to cause so much public distress after her loss was the doubt about the identity of who, and who was not, aboard her, for to keep father with son or pal with pal, men had swapped place with place in the camps from which the internees were being transferred, some wanting a transfer to they knew not where, while some were frightened of the unknown and only too anxious to stay put. Identities were temporarily exchanged; Pedro was called but Castellani turned up. Officialdom was too busy to do more than count heads.

The ship was torpedoed in the dawn of 2 July. Nearly 500 Italians were lost. So were 175 Germans. The horror of the sinking, the last hours of the lost, the ordeal of the survivors, have all been told many times.

The fact was that there was no really accurate record of the ship's complement.

Soho suffered its agonies of suspense, awaiting details and identities. But the ship itself was lost, swastika pennant below the red ensign at its masthead and all. The pennant indicated that she carried prisoners of war. She did; but in the ensuing weeks of confusion nobody seemed to know exactly who had gone down and who was saved. Soho was severely shocked, and mourned. The restaurant world of London lost its gaiety.

When eventually the four ships had delivered their human cargoes, the Australian and Canadian authorities seemed surprised. They had expected boatloads of Germans and pro-Germans. They could not understand that so many men wanted Kosher food. They could not understand that so many spoke good English, that so many had been born and educated in Britain. To people in the Dominions it just did not make sense.

Criticism of the transporting of aliens to the Dominions was sustained and intense. The A-class German internees sent abroad had mainly been collected early in the war: it was the sending of B- and C-class that caused the bitterness.

Writing so many years later, it could be said that the criticism seems deserved for many reasons. The Italians on the *Arandora Star*, many of whom were lost, were too often indiscriminately selected and not properly documented. In all cases where German As and POWs travelled on the same ship as refugees, the enemy servicemen had better accommodation and conditions. Refugees, especially Italian 'British', were attacked by Nazi Germans who should not have been allowed contact with them. Jewish refugees, who seem strange selections for transportation anyway, were similarly manhandled by the Nazis aboard. It was unnecessary for the refugees to be consigned to the holds of ships without deck exercise; their living-standards almost always seemed needlessly bad, that of the POWs uniformly good. In at least two instances—on the *Dunera* and the *Ettrick*—refugees had their belongings systematically stolen, and in the second case the Canadian Defence Department eventually admitted liability.

Exactly the percentage of refugees from Nazi oppression who suffered in all this is uncertain; what is certain is that the inefficiency and mistakes of war made it absurdly high.

3

The First Manx Camps

First official news that an internment camp would be created in the Isle of Man had been given the Manx in the local newspapers back in mid-May 1940. It was to be formed immediately, based on the Mooragh Promenade in Ramsey.

It would not be of huts as was Knockaloe in the 1914 war. In all, thirty houses were requisitioned and the occupants were ordered to get out by the end of the week. A promenade of small hotels and boarding-houses, ending with a miniature golf course, was to be enclosed by two rings of barbed wire fencing. Householders must leave their furniture but take personal belongings.

One of the island's leading newspapers, the *Mona's Herald*, greeted the internment scheme: it was a 'welcome indication' that at long last a move was being made towards replacing 'something of the losses entailed in the cessation of the visiting industry'. The tourists, it seemed, had disappeared; long live the replacements. The writer also pointed out that the island had a 'superfluity of milk and soon home-grown potatoes would be on the market'.

Things were on the move at last. The island people were having a thin time, a result of their semi-isolation. They manned no heavy industry, they made no munitions; they worked production lines that ended up as potatoes, not aircraft. Internment camps would mean some sort of work for many islanders.

And so it was. The Government Secretary advertised for chief storekeepers, chief clerks and male clerk-typists. All candidates had to be more than forty-one years old unless they had been rejected for military service.

Tenders were invited for a daily delivery of 500 pounds of bread, 240 pounds of meat on each of five days a week, 40 gallons of milk a day, and further tenders for potatoes, jam and sugar. Condiments and such items were required in lots of five hundredweights. All this for the Mooragh Camp.

On 21 May it was reported that the occupants along the promenade had now vacated the premises; they boarded themselves with the relatives and friends who were so numerous amongst the extended families on the Island. The furniture left had been valued, and pieces of rare or sentimental value had been removed by official permission. Beds used personally could be taken and second-hand ones substituted. Such was the local demand for used beds that they suddenly became almost unobtainable.

The activity at the northern extremity of Ramsey was intense; the hammering of pneumatic drills, a rare sound in those parts, disturbed the peace and brought sightseers to the town.

Hundreds of miles away at Dunkirk there was a hammering of a far more deadly sort. The Manx, in common with the rest of the King's subjects, listened with foreboding to the news. They were suddenly urged to carry their identity cards at all times.

The first sign of things to come was the arrival in Ramsey of the Steam Packet's ship *Rushen Castle*, with 150 troops and ten officers of the Royal Welch Fusiliers. They were the advance party, the men who were to be the military guard at the camp.

The first contingent of internees arrived the next day, on Monday evening, 27 May. They landed at Ramsey from the Belgian cross-Channel vessel the *Princess Josephine Charlotte*, a steamer of 1,140 tons, Master H. Aspislorch, which had brought them from Liverpool. The ship had been in Ostend harbour when the Low Countries were being overrun, and the collapsing regime in Brussels had ordered her to load with refugees and steam to Britain. This she did, arriving at Dover. There most of her crew and passengers were taken for investigation while the ship was ordered to Liverpool. She made several trips taking parties of aliens to internment.

Those were desperate days. The British authorities were taking no chances. Nothing could be taken at face value; an enemy alien could be a fifth columnist, an enemy agent or a saboteur. Equally, he could be a peaceful citizen, and most likely was. But the extremity of events justified drastic precautions; so said most official opinion.

In all 823 men reached the Isle of Man on that pleasant late spring evening. The youngest were schoolboys in shorts; only a few appeared to be anywhere near the age limit of sixty. The twenty-five to thirty-five age group predominated. As they came ashore on Ramsey's iron pier, they carried suitcases, small hand-luggage, parcels or even bundles on their backs. Once off the ship they were allowed to put heavier baggage on trolleys, and a number of men pushed the loads to the end of the pier. One internee was holding his portable typewriter while another carried his fishing-rod.

They were a mixed lot; some were poorly dressed and wore canvas shoes; others were well dressed and confident. One was leading his dog. They had been brought across under an armed guard, who disembarked first and were posted at intervals along the pier. It took an hour to complete the disembarkation, watched by a silent crowd who were kept at a distance by the police.

The onlookers noticed with interest that almost all the internees carried gas masks. These had not been generally issued on the island.

The *Ramsey Courier* reported that after 'a lengthy period of waiting' an officer appeared and called out: 'Can anyone speak English?' There was a general chorus that they could. The men were then ordered to march slowly to the camp and keep in a compact body. Accompanied by the armed guard, they were then taken along the promenade to the quay and over the swing bridge to the Mooragh.

The column, many whistling, made the short march or walk to the camp, where they were allotted to the various houses and given food. The military guard was already mounted. The sentries patrolled the boundaries of the compound. The gates closed; the camp itself was not to close until the summer of 1945, after the war in Europe had ended.

The Ramsey sightseers slowly dispersed, having watched the first aliens arrive. They were not allowed to loiter near the camp in the years ahead.

Only officials who met the ship would have been near enough to the pierhead to have heard what was surely one of the strangest orders ever issued by a British infantry officer. His rank and identity are not known. With troops he would have been at his ease, knowing precisely what to order and how to order it. Such was his training. But a large assortment of civilians, the fit and the frail, the middle-aged and the young, the rich and the poor, was different. They needed to be sorted out into some semblance of order, as required by the military mind.

The local paper later assured its readers that the officer carried out his work in a business-like manner and that his 'frequently repeated exhortation had the desired effect'.

He did not order 'Quick march,' nor did he yell out 'Get a move on.'

According to the report, his command was perhaps unique in the modern history of the British Army:

'Now, *please* get going.'

By the time Mooragh opened, authority was working at speed, not only on the mainland but on the island. Even as the first internees to be sent over—mainly B-category men recently collected—were looking around bewildered at Ramsey, it became known that another camp was being created on and behind the Central Promenade in Douglas. It would comprise forty or more houses, and the occupiers were to be out by 4 June.

The orders to householders were abrupt. They had to quit by 31 May. The arrangements were the same as had applied in Ramsey—the Manx Government would pay the rent and rates and make good any damage. The question of compensation would be considered later.

Suddenly it became known that 3,500 women were to be interned on the island and that the whole of Port Erin, a residential and holiday village on the west coast, had been taken over, along with its smaller neighbour Port St Mary. It was expected that the first batch would arrive that week.

The Manx Government Office said the women would not be restricted behind barbed wire, as in the male camps. Nor would boarding-house keepers and householders have to leave home; the arrivals would be billetees and would be catered for in the manner of ordinary holiday-makers but on a more modest scale. Such women would be able to keep their children with them.

A barrier was to be run up around the whole district, taking in a

golf course, tennis courts and swimming-pool. Special precautions would make sure that the internees did not leave the
confined area, and the village could only be entered by people on
business or those with permission; residents would need passes
to move in and out.

The Manx Government, it was revealed, had been left to
organize the camp. It was a rushed job and it was decided that,
until the barrier around Port Erin could be built, the roads into the
village would be closed and guarded.

Meanwhile the landladies who were to billet the women would
receive an allowance of £1. 1s. (£1. 5p.) a week. In modern
coinage it seems derisory. Even allowing for metrication,
inflation and the difference in the value of money in those days,
and then granting the notorious meanness of officialdom, it
seems very little. But to a seaside landlady with a house full of
empty rooms it was very welcome.

The first women arrived overnight on 29 May and disembarked
at Douglas from the *Princess Josephine Charlotte*. They started to
come ashore at seven in the morning and were sent on by train
across the island to Port Erin. Meanwhile the Belgian ship turned
round, returned to Liverpool, picked up more women and was
back again the following morning. She made one more round trip
to the island by the week-end and was never again entered in the
sailing-sheets of the Steam Packet Company.

4

A Question Mark

In the last week of June 1940 and the first half of July, 23,000 additional refugees were interned. Their numbers in the Isle of Man increased steadily, from fewer than 1,000 at the end of May, to roughly 8,500, excluding the women's camp, by the middle of July.

Almost all of them had spent time in one or more of the transit camps on the way to the island. There were at least a dozen such camps, some small and short-lived; in others men sometimes languished for many weeks. Among the larger ones, internees are most likely to remember Kempton Park, Ascot, Prees Heath, Huyton and Wharf Mills. This last, a derelict cotton mill near Bury, Lancashire, was almost certainly the worst of them all. The main building had a broken glass roof and rotting floors and was rat-infested. There was virtually no furniture; meals had to be eaten standing up. It was alleged that it housed 2,000 men with 500 others camping in the hall. Living-conditions were extremely primitive; the toilets were buckets, the medical facilities woefully inadequate.

The largest camp in England was probably that at Huyton in Lancashire, where Dr Hermann Scholz was to spend months. It consisted of an unfinished housing estate. At its worst it was said to be holding between 3,000 and 5,000 internees, many at one time in tents, with Nazis, pro-Nazis and Jews mixed up indiscriminately and dangerously. At first there were only straw sacks to sleep on. The camp started with only one doctor; four suicides were reported and there were two unsuccessful attempts. Many inmates suffered from mental disturbances, and nearly one in three internees was unfit.

Yet despite the unmade-up roads, the wet, the resentment and the bitterness, cultural and educational activities were started up by the Huyton inmates within the first few days of the camp opening. It had even happened on the *Dunera*. Such is the human spirit.

Kempton Park was one of the so-called transit stations out of the London region, and some thousands of B and C aliens passed through it, including Dr Scholz once again. They were billeted in the racecourse buildings, in the stables and in tents. Conditions were somewhat better than in many other camps; there was a sick bay with beds, and kosher food was available. Lingfield was another transit camp on a racecourse.

At Ascot the winter quarters of the Bertram Mills Circus had been taken over for temporary use. Conditions were unsatisfactory owing to lack of organization and preparation. Intakes of internees simply arrived seemingly without warning.

Prees Heath was in Shropshire, not far from Whitchurch. It was merely tented, hurriedly run up for the war emergency. There were no beds; internees slept on groundsheets. Luckily it was summer so conditions under canvas were bearable for the majority. There was criticism of the food, said to be inadequate and monotonous, and at one time the camp held rather more than 1,000 men. It was closed by the end of October.

There were many other internment camps, mostly for transits, mostly short-lived and mainly tented.

It was the haphazard nature of the internment of B and C men that caused the greatest hardship and brought out the strongest criticism from people who made it their business to investigate a subject about which little official news was forthcoming. They considered it absurd that men should be rounded up into uselessness when they had fled for their lives to Britain and were only too anxious to work for the allied war effort.

There was, of course, a reverse to the coin. The refugees who had crowded into Britain during the critical months before the war did not consist solely of industrious and harmless Jews who were escaping the Nazi clutches. Among them were political exiles who were on the run from Germany; they were a human rag-bag of idealists, revolutionaries and Communists of all sorts, among whom there would be the dubious and the desperate. In the eyes of authority, such people could be dangerous. The German Army was across the Channel; it was no time for taking chances.

The internees even included men who had been in Hitler concentration camps only a few months before they escaped to Britain. Others were sick, in some cases very sick.

It was a mess but, as men liked to remind each other, there was a war on.

However, compared with the mainland camps, the Isle of Man was to prove to be an orderly world flowing, if not with milk and honey, at least with milk.

In July 1940 a Parliamentary debate showed that public opinion was stirring. The nation was beginning to ask questions. Speakers argued that mass internment wasted war potential and was giving Britain a bad name overseas. The liberal attitude found a perhaps surprising supporter in Neville Chamberlain, then Lord President of the Council.

Reporting to the Cabinet on 18 July, he said that there were a large number of serious complaints about conditions in the camps and he was greatly disturbed. It had just been decided that the war value of an internee should not be the sole yardstick by which he could be released, and it was agreed that all men in the C category, thousands of whom had been arrested in the weeks of major crisis, could be freed.

Eventually, they were. Sometimes it took a long time.

5

Human Cargoes

The Isle of Man sent the best of its ships to the Dunkirk evacuation, bringing out 24,669 troops and losing three ships in the process. So one man in every fourteen who escaped from Dunkirk reached England in a Manx boat.

On the civilian front the frantic effort continued to equip the island for a chain of internment camps. The peacetime airfield was already being converted into a training base for the air arm of the Royal Navy, and two RAF stations were being built in the north of the island. The barbed wire slowly became the symbol of war from the ˙Ayres in the north down to Port St Mary in the south-west.

All through the final days of May the daily sailings from Liverpool brought more and more German women to the island, laconically listed as 'females' in the sailing-sheets of the Steam Packet Company. Then, on the following Tuesday, 4 June, the old *Victoria* sailed out from Liverpool, put in to Douglas and then went on to Ramsey, where it discharged its cargo of 401 internees; more men for Mooragh.

Three days later nearly 300 more German and Austrian women were brought over by the *Snaefell* to be entrained to Port Erin and Port St Mary, known in the records as Rushen Camp, that being the name of the sheading or district in which the two villages were situated.

Within days two more camps for men were opened in Douglas.

The *Rushen Castle* brought 1,003 internees on Tuesday, 11 June, the *Victoria* 200 men on the Thursday and 302 more on the Saturday. The *Rushen Castle* came from Liverpool on Friday with 1,010 men, turned round in the night, went back to the Mersey and reached Douglas once more on the Saturday afternoon with another 1,009. The men from these ships were drafted into the Onchan and Central camps, 1,200 in Onchan and nearly 1,000 in Central.

Onchan was the first camp in the Douglas area, and it had a sharp identity of its own. Its character was to change as the war developed but its basic structure remained unaltered, until it closed for the second and final time in November 1944. It consisted of sixty houses on a headland overlooking the sea, immediately beyond the northern end of the Douglas promenade. The site dominated the small electric railway terminal at sea-level below it, and looked down over Derby Castle. The wire enclosed parts of four roads, some of them with magnificent views of Douglas Bay. Eight houses in one road had four or five bedrooms, but most of the remainder had nine and two had sixteen; one even had thirty-two. It was boarding-house property of a superior Edwardian or late-Victorian type, and in view of its size and the fact that it had taken in land which included a football pitch and tennis courts, Onchan could reasonably have been regarded as the 'best' male internment camp on the island.

Central, which was opened within a few days of Onchan, was a much smaller and more concentrated unit, situated in thirty-four houses directly behind the Central Promenade roughly in the middle of the indented crescent of the bay. It held 2,000 men by the end of June, but inside ten months it had been emptied, and afterwards became an RAF station.

Within days in mid-June the number of male internees in the island virtually doubled, from 3,403 to 6,091. On Saturday, 22 June, the *Victoria* arrived from Liverpool with 193 men, and the *Rushen Castle* came in with 1,197 aliens, guarded by two officers and 75 other ranks. These men went quickly through the short police precautions required by the Manx authorities and were transferred at once to the new Palace Camp, which by the following week had become the most crowded of them all. This was situated in a prime position on the terrace over the main seafront; the small cliff that climbed behind it in picturesque fashion led up to the area known as Little Switzerland. Above was the Falcon

Cliff Hotel, overlooking much of the town; it was to play an important part in the life of the island's internees, for it was soon turned into their main hospital.

The camp consisted of twenty-eight houses above the front; they were sizeable private hotels or large boarding-houses, and by the end of June their number of internees had risen to 2,906, a figure from which it declined week by week. At the end of that month, too, the number of men held in the various Manx camps was more than 7,500.

Steadily the island's complex population mounted. Every incoming sailing brought with it servicemen, of whom a small number were for camp duties, but many more were for training; some were attached to administration departments now being transferred from the mainland; a few were on light duties after the rigours of the retreat in France. Naval personnel ranged from boy trainees and bandsmen to specialists undergoing secret training in new weaponry. Officers and other ranks of the RAF arrived to man and guard the two new flying-stations.

Most ships now brought in more and yet more internees. The Metropole Camp, mainly for Italians, opened in the first week of July, followed by Hutchinson. Both these were to stay open until 1944. Metropole, like Central and Palace, was on the front at Douglas, on the northern end of the promenade. It opened with 743 inmates, the number rising for a few months and dropping to below 650 by the end of the year.

The crew of the SS *Marzocco* were perhaps lucky. Had they reached the Isle of Man in the last hectic fortnight of June 1940, they would have been sent to Central or Palace Camp, which were both overcrowded. Mooragh and Onchan, the only other male camps open, were for Germans. But the crew came to Douglas in the first draft for the Metropole.

The men were still able to establish themselves as a unit. They were posted to the same house: Captain Marini was automatically appointed their house leader.

Giovanni Moneta took on the job of the daily food collection, drawing the rations from the camp's stores and sometimes cooking the meals. The men soon felt the absence of the pasta that they normally ate daily, but they were allowed to draw the flour and cook their own, so it soon appeared on the menu, and the crew were, if not happy, at least reasonably fed. The sea was right at the other side of the wire, the wind had a tang in it, and this was a very different life from Peterhead or Edinburgh Castle.

Dr Hermann Scholz was not so lucky; he was still at Huyton, a raucous community with a vehement Nazi element and a lot of internal bullying, a camp in which German seamen set up a system of discipline with which they dominated minority sections of the camp. The young doctor paid little attention. He shared a tent for two with three other inmates and did what he could to help the meagre medical service.

He was on the way to the Isle of Man. But as the weeks drifted into months and he still remained in the camp, with its unmade roads and its autumnal puddles, he realized that for him Huyton was not just a transit camp.

Hutchinson, where Scholz was eventually to languish, was behind the front promenade and took its name from a square of houses off Broadway, a road that wound upwards from the seafront to the back of the town. It opened in the second week of July with 415 internees, almost all German or Austrian. The figure jumped to 1,205 by the end of the month.

There was one more major camp to be opened. Peel was in many ways the most interesting of all, for it was eventually to contain the detainees, the men who ranked as a real danger. Many would come not from transit camps on the mainland but from prisons such as Brixton in London and Walton in Liverpool, in which some of them had been placed from the start for security reasons. Peel inmates would be the men who would be most likely to give any trouble. The camp started quietly enough, with ordinary internees, and at first it attracted little attention. It was not until months later that the Fascists and the trouble-makers were sent over from England.

The Manx newspapers were normally very free with their news about the island, and they did not hesitate to report on the camps. But the start at Peel, which was later to occupy so many sensational columns, went largely unrecorded. The island already had six camps, or seven counting the women in Rushen, so what appeared to be a rather small one over in Peel was hardly news. The first reference to the new camp was an entry, on 1 August, 1940, in the sailing-sheet of the Steam Packet Company. Against the *Ben-my-Chree* were the words: 'L to D 2.30 p.m.

Internees: 520 for Peel.' But the sailing-sheet was circulated privately.

This brought the number of male internees in the Manx camps at the start of August to approximately 9,700.

The figure was to be exceeded on 8 August, when it was 10,024, the highest total it ever reached. This, with the camp at Port Erin where there were approaching 4,000 women and children, gives a maximum total of about 14,000.

The figure of 10,024 may be taken as accurate; it comes from the surviving records in the Manx Museum of the Internment Camps Division of the local government offices. The men's total had been 9,761 on 3 August and 9,988 on 10 August, after which it declined steadily. The estimate of the maximum number of women in the south of the island is approximate. On the last day of 1940 local records showed 3,134 along with four males in the Rushen area and added that 849 had already been released. This makes it reasonable to put the maximum all-island figure at any one time as no higher than 14,000. Larger figures have been suggested; Manx records do not support them.

It was by no means a one-way traffic. A trickle of releases had started from the very beginning as individual cases were examined, and men—usually wanted on important war work— were sent back to the mainland. Sometimes internees were released by transfer; the day before the *Ben-my-Chree* brought the first arrivals for Peel, the same ship returned 250 aliens on its outward voyage to Liverpool. A month earlier the *Tynwald*, back temporarily from outstanding war service at Dunkirk, had left Douglas for Glasgow carrying 1,200 internees, presumably to be trans-shipped to one of the Dominions, where many of them spent the war. Some were known to be on the *Arandora Star* and were lost.

Other camps were planned for men on the island, but they were short-lived. The Granville and the Regent were on the Douglas front, at the southern end near the harbour. They were eventually taken over by the Royal Navy and became HMS *Valkyrie*, a shore training establishment. Granville lasted a year from October 1940. It had an establishment for 750 inmates but only briefly approached that figure. Regent had an allocation for 700 internees; it appears never to have had any at all. Falcon Camp, above Palace Camp, was also surplus to requirements. It is likely that Regent and Falcon were groups of properties commandeered in the emergency before the internment policy was modified in July. The Sefton was a camp for only a few months; it was created late in 1940 and had vanished from the list by March 1941. It was a prime site, surrounding an hotel on the front.

Ignoring Regent and Falcon, there were in all nine camps for men on the Isle of Man: Mooragh at Ramsey, Peveril at Peel, Onchan just outside the town boundary of Douglas, and six in Douglas itself, of which Central, Palace, Metropole and Hutchinson were the largest, with Granville and Sefton the smallest. To these must be added Rushen, the sheading in which Port St Mary and Port Erin are situated. Here were the women's and later the married camps which for administration purposes ranked as one, making ten units in all.

6

The Women Arrive

By the end of May 1940 nearly 4,000 women had started to arrive on the Isle of Man for internment. Some of them had been quartered briefly in women's prisons on the mainland before they crossed over. In this experience they were even unluckier than most of the male internees, comparatively few of whom had been through a prison, although some might well have preferred that experience to the deplorable conditions at Wharf Mills. A small number of women had been on a War Office wanted list prepared earlier against the event of war. These had been sent to women's prisons at the start, and they were the victims of hostility from other prisoners, for they had the standing of prisoners of war, which gave them a certain status along with greater freedom of movement inside the gaol.

A few women in Class C were interned at first, but the great majority were in B and some brought their children with them. Some were pregnant. They reached the island at the end of a long and unpleasant journey; apart from their assembly in places like Holloway, many had spent some days in prisons and hostels in the Liverpool area and had been jeered at on their way to the docks. The automatic internment of C-category women was stopped after only ten days.

From Douglas the new arrivals were taken on to Port Erin by train and were then assembled in St Catherine's Church Hall, near the railway station. There they met the first of the Home Office representatives who were to look after them.

At the start conditions were disorganized. The staff for the entire camp consisted of a Commandant and five assistants, suddenly called on to handle this influx of apprehensive and excited women. It was an abrupt transformation, as startling to the people of the small holiday resort as it was to the camp authorities who had to deal with the internees as best they could. For in a matter of a few days the population of Port Erin had more than doubled. There were now nearly two internees to every resident. Suddenly they brought the thinned-out streets to life; they mostly talked in a foreign language, and talked excitedly. They brought a new noise to Port Erin and, to a lesser extent, to Port St Mary, which was even smaller.

The internees were allotted to hotels or houses and sent on their way with rough directions of how to get there. Although the camp site was to cover fifteen square miles, the built-up area was small, and many Port Erin residents today can remember seeing the first arrivals walking slowly down the road in twos and threes looking bewildered at the unfamiliar scene, the road names incomprehensible in the Manx language.

Many of the women were in poor condition; they were very frightened. Their past had been torn away, their men had been snatched from them, and in many cases their children had been left behind. The refugee associations that had befriended them and had often brought them out of Germany and central Europe, were now hundreds of miles distant in a London that was threatened as it had never been threatened before. To these women the prospect was fearful. For some others the reaction was different. The patriotic Germans among them were resentful, sullen and determined to be difficult. They had no love for Britain, and their hearts were in their fatherland.

The Jewish and anti-Nazi women were in the majority, but the pro-Nazis were more vocal; the language was what the two sides had most in common. The internees were mostly nurses, students and domestic servants, with some theatricals, a designer or two, working Germans from various business houses, and internees who were married to Germans. Some of the wives were British by birth; some had made their homes in Britain but were indifferent to the war. Some of the domestics had been professional women who could more easily get a work permit by registering as servants.

Apart from all these, there were noticeably well-dressed women from the oldest of professions. They arrived at Port Erin in small numbers. Eventually there were about 150 of them, disliked by the other internees, who asked for them to be housed separately. Most of them ended up in one hotel. They made very little trouble.

Sometimes there would be a flare-up of spite between Nazis and Jewesses in the camp, but such things were usually of a minor nature. In all, Port Erin saw little of the open hatred that broke out into fighting in the men's camps.

Being caterers in the holiday trade, the boarding-house owners knew how to handle newcomers. The women were quickly taken over, allotted their rooms, almost all of them sharing; anything like a single room was unlikely, at least until things had been finally organized, but by the morning after the first main arrival arrangements had to be made all over again. The internees had started to sort themselves out; pairings were changed around; a girl on the third floor now suddenly occupied a shared room on the first; there were even changes between the houses, discovered only slowly by the puzzled landladies, who had to report it all to the camp office.

Many of the women were quick to become customers of the local banks, of which the Isle of Man Bank was the principal. Some had brought their valuables, some a substantial amount of cash. On the afternoon of their arrival and on the following day they were busy becoming customers. They deposited jewellery; one even lodged valuable furs; in all scores of them opened accounts, often for very small amounts.

In the weeks to come there was a spectacular spending-spree, a harvest for the shopkeepers, an irritation to the Manx, who did not like the ostentatious buying. Reports of the spendthrift, sunbathing German women even reached the London newspapers. The authorities eventually developed a system, designed to help the internee as much as anyone: the camp started its own bank, managed by a chartered accountant from Douglas, C. R. Ducker, who was called in to the camp office and found a safe filled with cash in spills of screwed-up paper bearing the name of the individual internee. He evolved a system: the shopper would collect her bills, take them to the camp bank, which would produce the cash if she had it and return the bill, with which the internee would go back to the shops and claim the goods, the camp meanwhile debiting the woman's account.

The camp bank was also where money earned by the women was allotted and paid to them. Most of the accounts with the local banks had been cleared out soon after the start, spent on the shopping-sprees.

One woman, a remarkable one at that, was in charge of the camp. Dame Joanna Cruickshank had had a fine career in a highly specialized field. She was sixty-four years of age and had held very senior appointments in the nursing world for many years. Originally trained at Guy's Hospital, London, she had served in the First World War, rising to be Matron-in-Chief of Princess Mary's RAF Nursing Service. She had been Matron-in-Chief of the British Red Cross and then of the War Organization of the British Red Cross and the Order of St John. It was a splendid record of committee-room successes, based on vast practical experience in the field of nursing administration. Now she came to the island as Commandant of the women's camp.

She was a single-minded woman who took no particular trouble to make friends; she had a job to do and she did it with devotion. If, in the course of carrying it out, there was a corn to be trodden on, then someone might yelp. It was a small matter. She possessed a strong personality and many virtues. She could not possibly have had her long string of professional successes had she been otherwise. But hers had always been a well-ordered world, and improvisation was new to her. No one would have been better at supervising the welfare of 4,000 patients neatly arranged in hospital beds; but the same patients forever restless and arguing ceaselessly in a foreign tongue were another matter, and a problem she was quite inexperienced to tackle. She was also a woman of strong prejudices.

It was said of her that the Dame preferred women around her; she did not work easily with men. She certainly did not endear herself to the Manx officials with whom it was necessary for her to have contact. They saw her as a precise, well-laundered builder of a personal empire, doing everything to the order of a well-thumbed rule book, where one existed. At anything unexpected, anything outside her experience, she hesitated and fell back on an occasional bluster. She was not the sort of administrator who made mistakes and she had no time for those who did. Her reputation grew in the island; she was regarded as something of a martinet. It was wise to be careful.

Martinet she may have been but her task was to look after the

welfare of her women, and this she did with dedication. It was
near her own specialized subject. She listened to the advice of an
experienced Quaker welfare officer named Bertha Bracey who
was the first arrival from any welfare organization. She agreed
that an official staff of six was absurdly inadequate to deal with
the developing problems of Port Erin, and she immediately
approved invitations to the Jewish Refugees Committee in
London for two experienced voluntary workers to come over,
and to the Society of Friends to send three more. By the time the
women's camp had reached its capacity, Dame Joanna's own
staff had increased to about twenty-five, and it was possible for
most but not all of the voluntary workers to return to the mainland.

The Dame agreed to the suggestion that Margaret Collyer
should continue living in and helping in the camp. Miss Collyer
was a Quaker worker attached to the GEC—the Germany Emergency Committee—of the Society of Friends, and she had already
done active work in Berlin and Amsterdam. As German was the
majority language of the camp, her German experience was
particularly valuable.

On the surface Port Erin and Port St Mary looked anything but
internment centres. It was a fine summer and the women were
free to shop, swim or sunbathe as they wished. They bought
sunglasses, they combed through the shops for sweets and minor
delicacies. They almost cleared out the drapery shops. Any
length of material was in demand. There was a curfew, but there
were restrictions. Internees were supposed not to talk to the
menfolk of the district. They were supposed to do domestic work
in their houses, but if this was internment, then it was a very
different thing from Holloway.

There was much swimming, and a few women swam in the
nude. This would have caused no comment in Scandinavia but
occasioned no little passing interest in the south of the Isle of
Man, which was not used to such candour. News of this friendly
disclosure passed rapidly around the island.

Entry to the Rushen Camp was strictly barred; while the wire
had not yet been erected, all roads were marked and guarded and
admission was by special pass only. It was hard to get in; for the
people who lived there it was all a nuisance; they had to be
supplied with special passes in addition to their identity cards.
They did not like it.

While the weather lasted, so did the swimming, and one legend resulted. It was widely said that a small party swam out to an Irish fishing-boat that was anchored offshore and thus escaped to Ireland. This was simply not true, and the women were alleged to have sent rude postcards to Dame Joanna. There were no such postcards, of course, just as there was precious little nude bathing. These things get greatly over-stated. The fact was that there had been a British raid on the Norwegian Lofoten Islands, and a number of people had been brought back for interrogation wearing no more than they stood up in. Hence the swimming nudity. And hence, too, a rapid supply of swimsuits.

Margaret Collyer, the Quaker, later wrote that the beautiful weather and the novelty helped to balance the difficulties of the early days, but the bright face of things on the front at Port Erin hardly suggested what lay behind. She stressed the keen personal anxiety about absent children and relatives, the sense of injury at suddenly being interned, the renewed feeling of insecurity, the incompatibility of individuals, the increasing lack of money, of possessions and of work. She did not mention the frustration felt by a woman if her man was only a dozen miles away in another Manx camp but was much more distant through the post and an eternity through the officialdom of war.

Inevitably any suggestion that an internee was reasonably comfortable drew angry comment from some quarters, including a few critics in the island. There was sniping in the columns of the local newspapers; there was sniping in Tynwald, the island's Parliament. But it was mainly unimportant. There was also criticism away in Westminster, in the House of Commons. The argument was that the internment regulations did not go far enough. Members alleged that there was much resentment in the Isle of Man that alien women were living in hotels and boarding-houses at a cost to the country of a guinea a week apiece, while the wives of ordinary soldiers had to make do with 17 shillings plus a miserable 7 shillings docked weekly from their husband's pay. In the national Press the *Daily Mail* had been leading the way with descriptions of the pleasures of internment, with golf, sea-bathing and cinema shows for the aliens.

It all made good copy. The war itself made gloomy news.

Order slowly emerged during the early days at Port Erin and Port St Mary. The landladies did stalwart work. Each hotel or house organized its own rota and divided its workload between the inmates. One of the larger hotels had 65 bedrooms and 120 internees, every one of whom was responsible for cleaning and maintaining the room she shared. Inmates took it in turns to clean the corridor on which they lived. Each floor had an internee in charge of allocating bathtime. Cleaning the public rooms and the dining-room, and waiting at table, were all done by organized turn. All these duties were unpaid. Cooking was different. It earned money.

Payment for work done outside normal housework was a matter that involved the Protecting Power, the neutral state which in international usage looked after the interest of interned nationals of the country it represented. In the case of the Germans this Power was Switzerland and to the Swiss fell the responsibility of agreeing the rate for paid work in the camp and nature of it. The rate of 10d. a day was struck; later it was doubled.

Cooking for 120 inmates, for instance, was more than normal housework, so the cooks were paid. It was better to have good food than have it ruined by working a rota of burned potatoes. Six cooks were chosen from the women at the Golf Links, which was a typical hotel, and they did one week on and two weeks off, earning their 10d. a day one week in three. Fuelling, stoking and maintaining the central boiler for hot water were all considered heavy work and were also paid, the money being handed in at the camp bank, where it would go to the credit of the internee. The responsibility for payment rested with the hotel-keeper, but the camp office expected proprietors not to exceed the standard rate by passing a little coin to the internee direct.

One order had to be strictly obeyed throughout Port Erin at all times. Curfew was at nine o'clock in the evening during the summer days and would be at five o'clock in the winter. This routine was followed in modified form by every hotel and house in the village.

So it was that by the end of May 1940 Home Secretary Sir John Anderson was able to tell Parliament that 3,200 women between the ages of sixteen and sixty had been interned. Unknown to him some were older. It was not until November that he gave the figures once more; this time it was nearly 4,000, of whom 300 were pregnant.

The women had a mutual enemy: boredom. There was at first nothing to do. They were not even obliged to get up in the morning if they did not want to.

Steadily Dame Joanna, aided by voluntary welfare workers, improved all this. Boredom gave a woman time in which to brood on her distress, to see her problems, which were real enough, at their very worst. Boredom was the mother of depression, and depression could lead to desperation. The camp was only three weeks old when the small Port Erin police station recorded two incidents: a women alien of sixty-seven had to be certified and sent off to the island's mental hospital at Braddan, now generally referred to as Ballamona; a few days later a fifty-two-year-old woman was removed to the same place. The stress was showing. The first suicide was not for some months.

The boredom and the depression had other consequences. Women became quarrelsome, changing their rooms and even their houses regularly; some became light-fingered, and pilfering increased. Lesbian relationships were formed, but they called for no special action by authority.

Slowly the women were sorted out. A form was circulated on which applicants could apply for repatriation. Those who signed it were put together in houses on their own. They were the pro-Nazis, and if they took an oath and signed their support of the Third Reich, they would even secure a small amount of pocket money, which would reach them once a quarter from Germany through the Swiss representatives in London. Sister Anna Jochmann, who was camp leader and who had formerly been Matron of the German Hospital at Dalston in East London, was given the responsibility of dealing with 'the German Money', as the internees called it; it took time to get all this organized and started. Eventually the Golf Links was filled with Nazi women, while the Windsor, a somewhat smaller place, had the forty-five nursing sisters from the German Hospital, who had also signed the pro-Nazi declaration. These internees who opted for repatriation were almost all to spend the next four years on the Isle of Man.

The nurses were often deaconesses of the Lutheran Church. They always held a morning service and later managed to 'print' their own hymn book. Back in London they had been abruptly collected while at their hospital routine. One nurse actually told her landlady that she was taken off to internment while her patient was still in the bath.

For all the women in those early days there was little work, and for most there was by now no money. That was the life at the start; the knitters merely unpicked that which they had finished and started to knit all over again. It helped to pass the time. Such helpers as became available set about putting this right. They helped to organize a clothing department, where parcels coming through from the various welfare organizations could be sorted and distributed: some tried to deal with the minor needs of the penniless from their funds.

In the autumn there occurred a great boost to morale throughout the camp. Even the single women who had no children of their own rejoiced at the arrival of those of other refugees, who had been obliged to leave them behind on the mainland in the frenzied rush into internment during the great crisis at the end of May. It was true that some children had come over with their mothers in the first drafts from Liverpool, but where hurried arrangements for its welfare could be made, a child was likely to be left behind. The mothers who were interned grew increasingly anxious. They wanted the children badly, and it was realized that on humanitarian grounds it was better all round for the family to be reunited, even in the Rushen Camp. Many families were registered with the Jewish Refugees Committee, which was the active wing of the Central British Fund for World Jewish Relief, or with the Friends Committee for Refugees and Aliens. These were the two principal organizations connected with the welfare of internees.

Arrangements to bring over children who had been left behind were made by the camp authorities; approximately fifty children, some of whom were not Jewish, were assembled in London along with a dozen adults. The party was in the charge of Joan Stiebel, who was a secretary of the Jewish Refugees Committee.

The journey was nothing if not eventful as the group included two small babies who were only a few months old. The party travelled by train from Euston to Liverpool and spent the night at an evacuated children's hospital, the adults listening to an air raid, of which the seaport had many. They crossed to Douglas the next day and had to walk from the ship to the railway station carrying some very substantial toddlers who could not manage the distance along the North Quay. They were then locked into the carriages and arrived at Port Erin, at first unable to get out of the train. When they were unlocked, they could not move on the platform for the milling mass of internees, who had turned up to greet them in a babble of anticipation. Any contact from the outside world was exciting. The arrival of children, accompanied by people from the distant welfare organizations, was an enormous solace to women who had known despair.

At about this time it was realized that a kindergarten was needed for the older children. And if the war went on wearily for a long time, something more than a kindergarten would be required. A start was made. In late September an internee, using trestle tables and forms as the only furniture, started a class in a small room in St Catherine's Church Hall.

Soon it was too crowded and moved on to a larger room in Dandy Hill. It had no qualified teachers, only enthusiasts among the internees; but at about the time of the move a new contingent arrived from their temporary quarters in Holloway. They included some very experienced Montessori teachers led by Dr Minna Specht, whose own school back in Germany had been exiled to Denmark, and then to Britain. She and her colleagues took over the small unit and developed it.

Talks took place with Dame Joanna, who appears not to have delayed her decision. The camp must take advantage of its own skills. They were to go ahead. The school developed with increased enthusiasm. Educational and occupational work for adults developed steadily. The school moved on to Collinson's Café, going later to two houses where classes could be held in separate rooms. Lessons now started in English, with a supply of printed textbooks. These English classes were particularly well attended. Classes were also launched in philosophy, languages, mathematics and other subjects.

Practical classes were also introduced. Spinning, weaving and dressmaking were taught, and a library was set up based on books donated by welfare organizations. Recalling this later, Margaret Collyer wrote how the librarian was a Jewish internee and she had as her assistant the wife of a Nazi. They worked together seemingly amicably.

So conditions in the Rushen Camp and the mood of the women in it improved steadily. Those internees who now had their children with them were spared one of their keenest personal anxieties. But despite the study and training classes there were still far too many empty hours in the day for far too many women.

The scheme for a Service Exchange has been largely credited to

Ruth Borchardt, an internee whose identity raises a question mark. Her paper 'The Service Exchange in an internment camp' was published by the Society of Friends in 1943 and was awarded a prize—by the Joseph Rowntree Charitable Trust—for an essay on lessons to be learned from the work of wartime relief service. Her writing shows that she certainly knew her subject well, but she was not a Friend. Nor was she known to the Jewish Refugees Committee or any of the Jewish organizations contacted by the author. Significantly, no record survives of a Ruth Borchardt in any Manx files, so exactly who she was is something of a mystery. Possibly she used a pseudonym. She could have been a married woman with a husband in one of the men's camps and preferred to write under her maiden name.

According to Ruth Borchardt's own reportage, she and some fellow internees argued that morale could be kept up only if the women were kept busy. Internees were anxious to work and would prefer it to accepting charity in the way of clothing. They had no funds apart from the welfare organizations, but it was argued that 'service tokens' could be given in exchange for work done; these would entitle the holder to other services supplied by other token-earners, to goods manufactured inside an exchange system and to communal services such as the lending library, concerts and even one day, it was hoped, a café. It was better, argued Ruth Borchardt, for a woman to exchange her best for what others could do better. 'Thus, boldly, we set out to create no less than an artificial economy,' she wrote, surveying what she saw as an important social experiment.

The first outsider to see the virtue of the idea was Margaret Collyer. The range of the operation, the various services it could cover, the many goods it could make, was sketched out, and the problem of how to get started discussed at length. Then, after a month of preparation, it was necessary to get the approval of authority. Perhaps a little to the surprise of some of the women, Dame Joanna gave her backing at once. It was worth trying. In London the Home Office had been saying that the internees should be given work; the camp staff was too busy to organize such things. Let the women do it themselves.

Some thousands of tokens were minted by the simple process of cutting out small coin-sized squares of cardboard from cornflake packets and stamping the camp's name on them. Then, on 19 September, 1940, a notice was posted asking for volunteers for dress- and underwear-making, sewing, cutting, laundry work, hairdressing and beauty culture, garden work, handicraft, carpentry, wood-chopping and salvage-collecting.

Within two weeks there were 1,200 volunteers.

The Commandant allowed the use of a small empty room as an office and gave a modest supply of equipment and tools. The enthusiasts who led the movement managed to contribute £2 in real money to purchase the first materials. In little more than another month a hairdressing and beauty parlour had started in what had been a men's lavatory in one of the larger hotels. A laundry was busy within six weeks. Gardeners extended the allotment originally started by Quaker welfare workers. Cutters worked in a room next to the office. But basic equipment was always sparse. The women had only one sewing-machine between them, and the brassière- and corset-makers used it for an hour a day. There were arguments in plenty. Cutting-room work was taken away to be finished at home and then returned for inspection, as was millinery. Work was doled out to the knitters. At least they did not need a machine. After some persuasion the Exchange even managed to secure premises that made a shop of sorts, and the two carpenters who had joined the band of enthusiasts managed to fit it out from some old wooden boxes.

The women were keen, very keen; a branch Exchange was opened in Port St Mary. It was soon independent of Port Erin, but internees could spend their tokens at either shop. There was never enough work to go round, so employment was not allowed to exceed six half-days a week. Half a day's work was paid for by two tokens—regardless of the effort or skill involved. No attempt was made to copy a wage scale from real life; too many arguments would have resulted. However, some difficulties arose when a number of the more skilled workers argued for more than the two tokens given, say, to a salvage-collector.

This inevitably led to a miniature black market. Costume tailors sometimes preferred to work for internees who could still pay real money for the end product. Some worked up a connection with customers 'outside'—very much against the rules. But, according to Ruth Borchardt, many women devoted their time to the Exchange, accepting the satisfaction of communal work and enjoying the fun of co-operating as part of their wages.

Obviously there were troubles. Some internees could not

understand that the Exchange had to put back what little money it earned from sales to the purchase of new raw materials. By late November 1940, it seemed that a crisis was approaching. Then, as Christmas neared, the store of handicraft knick-knacks that had been piled up suddenly started selling in spectacular fashion. Even the people outside the camp managed to buy some of the output as souvenirs and presents.

Dame Joanna Cruickshank did eventually ensure some sort of backing in real money for the Exchange tokens. She arranged that if an internee had earned twenty-four tokens in a fortnight, which at two a session was the maximum income possible, then eight tokens could be exchanged for 2s. 3d. pocket money in cash, which the Commandant obtained from the Home Office Employment Fund. The fact that these coupons could be turned in for cash, however small, increased the internees' trust in the scheme. The cashing of roughly a third of the tokens for a driblet of money also helped to take the strain off a currency system that was backed by little but optimism.

The scarcity of tools and equipment, due to the absence of substantial cash in hand, prevented the scheme from developing. At its busiest it employed more than a thousand women; it lifted them temporarily from introspection and depression. Unfortunately, lack of facilities meant that it was never able to give work to all the internees who applied to join it. At best work was found for forty-three per cent of the applicants, and many of those could only be employed part-time.

Two gradual processes finally killed the scheme. Tribunals had started to sit in Douglas to consider the release of internees; at the same time the shortage of material throughout Britain more and more restricted work of this sort. Vitally, the prospect, amounting steadily to the likelihood, of release changed the general mood; there was now a focal point of hope. At about the time when the Exchange Scheme was at its busiest and most successful, around December 1940, the main releases were starting. Key workers disappeared back to the pierhead at Douglas and to liberty; newcomers had to be trained but lacked the old enthusiasm. As Ruth Borchardt wrote, the women did not take the work so seriously any more; real life was beckoning.

The Exchange ran down just as did the population of the camp. In November 1941 the scheme was formally wound up; it had found work for idle hands, provided services and created goods in exchange for small pieces of cornflake packets. The token had by then been stabilized at a real 3d., and all those outstanding were redeemed in cash at the closure. The small makeshift workshops that had been created were taken over by the camp authorities.

It is fair to say that at least one reputable observer with a long memory is sceptical about the Borchardt report. It is well remembered that by the end of May 1941, when major changes took place in the Port Erin administration, the scheme had broken down with masses of valueless token money in circulation. It had been a good idea but it had outlived its purpose and was wound up, allegedly some months before the date given in the report to the Friends. In its place there was substituted a simple scheme whereby items made by the internees were paid for with cash, the woman receiving the fixed rate of 1s. 8d. a day, which was the amount by then agreed for internees working on farms.

By the time the exchange scheme had run its course, the face of the greater map had changed. The war was now worldwide. The little world in the south-west corner of the Isle of Man had changed, too. Dame Joanna Cruickshank had gone.

7

Settling In

In the early days the life in the men's camps on the Isle of Man depended largely on two things—the nationality of the inmates and the personality of the camp commander. A pioneer at the time of the very first arrivals was the commander of all the camps, Lieutenant-Colonel S. W. Slatter. It was he who had received the men off the steamer at Ramsey. He was typical of the camp officers at the start of the internment operation. He had served in the First World War, having been commissioned at the end of 1916, when he was posted to the Duke of Cambridge's Own, the Middlesex Regiment.

He did not remain in the service after the war, but on the outbreak of the next one he was given a Regular Army Emergency Commission with the rank of Temporary Major. He became an Acting Lieutenant-Colonel at the end of May 1940. He vanished from the Army List after February 1941. During his Second War service he was listed as 'specially employed'. He was almost certainly too old for fighting service, and his somewhat brief war work probably reached its peak with his camp command.

The camp officers generally were either veterans in military terms or had been given relatively light duties after wounds or illness while on active service. In the course of the war there was a considerable number of camp commanders and adjutants, and some scores of junior officers. There were only three commandants—that is, officers senior to commanders. Following Slatter there was Lieutenant-Colonel R. Baggalay. He was succeeded by Lieutenant-Colonel A. M. Scott. Theirs was the ultimate local responsibility for the running of the men's camps.

At the start of internment a notice in English and German assured all arrivals that nothing avoidable would be done to add to their discomfort or unhappiness. If men were to live together successfully, there had to be a code of discipline. The code, it was stated, would be obeyed: there would be no aggression. Notices concluded: 'The measure of your co-operation and behaviour will decide the measure of your privileges and the consideration shown for your welfare. In all events, you are assured of justice.' So said Colonel Slatter.

The discipline was simple. The immediate camp commander could award up to twenty-eight days' punishment for what was essentially a camp offence, and all camps had small detention units; Metropole, for instance, had six cells near its guardroom. 'Crimes' were mainly trivial; fighting among internees was stamped on, and anyone guilty could expect fourteen days; wilful damage, breaking the black-out and insubordination were all punishable by decree of the commander at the morning parade. These were internal matters, calling for no reference to the police. Others were different.

The Manx police had no jurisdiction inside the camps, but they could be, and were, called in over more serious matters, such as an incident involving grievous bodily harm or a felony where something more than twenty-eight days' detention could be involved. These were matters involving the law of the land.

Escape attempts, when they did not get beyond the camp's own guards, were handled internally and it might seem leniently, for they usually received no more than a fortnight's detention. But where an internee broke free of the camp, he was in Manx territory then it became a police matter; if caught, he would be returned to his camp but prosecuted for any misdemeanour committed while at liberty—the theft of a rowing-boat in an attempt to get away, or whatever. He would then come before the civil courts, who would send him to prison in Douglas before returning him to his sorrowing commander.

Over in the women's camp Dame Joanna had similar disciplinary powers. Those of her women who received detention sentences were usually sent to the Port Erin or the Port St Mary police stations. As such they would come into civilian records. Papers suggest that a punishment of twenty-eight days was allowed but never given at Rushen.

Once on the Isle of Man, the internees found that the postal conditions, while still frustrating and inadequate, were somewhat better than in the mainland camps, where letters often took a month or more in transit. A major area of complaint was thus improved. Yet at first letters between Douglas and the interned women at Port Erin did take a long time, and this caused needless irritation and anxiety. These postal delays had from the beginning been a desperate grievance to the internees. Now, as the administration of the Manx camps consolidated, a central post office for all internee mail was set up in Douglas, and the post was handled much more speedily. All incoming mail was censored at Liverpool, where sometimes mailbags piled up in hundreds. Outgoing mail from the Manx camps was read by local intelligence officers with comparatively little delay, but the incoming was still sent through Liverpool, where it had to be vetted before it could go on to the island.

Internees used the mail as a means of getting their complaints to the authorities. A serious moan attracted the attention of the censor, who passed it on to higher quarters, through whom the camp commander learned of the grievance.

Letter-smuggling went on particularly in the early days and especially from the women's camp. From the beginning there had been a trickle of internees who were liberated back to the mainland. These people, and visitors who were allowed to come to the camps later on, could bring out uncensored letters to be posted off the island. If caught by the police at the pier head or by officials at the camp, they would be prosecuted in the civil court and sent to the island's prison.

The more intelligent internees had another serious complaint. They were starved of news; newspapers and the radio were at first denied them. This made the camps hotbeds of rumour, exploited by the anti-British elements who proclaimed that the invasion had started. However, serious journals and newspapers were steadily allowed and more popular papers soon followed in some. At Mooragh the newspaper readers were catered for from the start, for on 4 June the Ramsey police advised their headquarters that thirty-six copies of the *Daily Mail* were delivered to the camp daily and that thirty-six copies of the *Ramsey Courier* were also on order. But Mooragh was the exception.

After a few weeks, excerpts from BBC broadcasts were allowed at the discretion of the camp commanders, sometimes relayed live, sometimes reported later on the internal loudspeaker system.

In all this the women at Rushen were very much luckier. They found the houses where they could hear the radio. Personal sets were strictly forbidden, and later in the war receivers in public rooms were adapted so that only BBC programmes could be picked up.

Fred Uhlman, the artist and writer who was interned in the Hutchinson Camp and who gives a vivid picture of it in his autobiography, made the point that it was not the men with the greatest intelligence who best resisted the depression caused by barbed wire, the boredom and the lack of privacy. The dullards took it all much more lightly; they were housed, they were fed, they were safe. They sat in the sun when there was sunshine, they played cards, and the war went on far, far away.

It was the man with imagination who really suffered. He worried about his wife, he worried about his family, his home, his work, his plight as an internee, and in all probability he resented his position as an injustice. He never knew when he would be free again. If he was a Jew, he had an extra worry: the double hazard in which he and his family were placed. For not only did he face the common danger, but if he lived and the Nazis won, he and his family would be singled out for destruction. In some camps he would be in physical danger from the Nazi element, although the two sides were kept apart as far as possible.

The pro-Nazi Germans in the camps would do nothing to help the British war effort. Sometimes they were businessmen or professionals who had been caught up in the enemy net; many of them had no particular bitterness but they were German. It was the fortune of war. The mass of anti-Nazis, Jews of German and Austrian extraction and political zealots of the far Left were the men with the deeper sense of grievance against internment, some only too anxious to serve in the forces if they were young enough, or else in their professional or craft capacities.

Order gradually emerged. There was a driblet of release right from the earliest days as successful applications, sometimes from outside the camp, were made to the authorities. As the months went by, internees could volunteer for war work and in many cases were released to make their contribution. Many had been busy on important war work when they were pulled into internment.

As in the women's camp, applicants for repatriation were put on a different footing from the rest, were plainly pro-Nazi and received pocket-money through Switzerland. Repatriation was in fact slow in coming. Dr Scholz is an example: he was arrested in the first days of the invasion scare, spent depressing months in the mainland camps before getting to Hutchinson in Douglas and applied formally to be repatriated as soon as the form was there to be filled in. Even so, he only reached Germany some months after the war was over.

The yearning for release was generally desperate. There was always the hope that a plea to the right man at the right moment could do the trick, and internees spent a great deal of their time in the early days writing letters, often to complete strangers who might just possibly be influential.

There was one way that offered the younger, fitter men a reasonable hope of an escape route—non-combative work in what had once been the old Labour Corps of the First World War, now reformed to the Auxiliary Military Pioneer Corps. Churchill himself was believed to favour the idea that the 'enemy alien' could help behind the lines, and there developed a steady movement from the camps to the Army.

Many of the male internees fretted at the lack of immediate work. The professionals and the educated class generally went in for concentrated study. They taught what they knew and learned what they could. Lectures and teaching classes had started in the despondency of the mainland camps. On the Isle of Man, where conditions were much better, they opened up almost at once. Soon most camps had their 'Open University' and were proud of it. The most brilliant collection of internees was in Hutchinson, officially known as P camp, where it was said that at one time there were thirty university professors and lecturers. Some were men of international standing, and their internment was a temporary waste of talent. Hutchinson with its almost exclusively German and Jewish population, produced a memorable sentence in Uhlman's memoirs. He wrote: 'Every evening one could see the same procession of hundreds of internees, each carrying his chair to one of the lectures, and the memory of all these men in pursuit of knowledge is one of the most moving and encouraging that I brought back from the strange microcosm in which I lived for so many months.'

Hutchinson had few musicians compared with Onchan, but it did have Marian Rawicz, highly successful member of the Rawicz and Landauer piano duo. Landauer was later transferred from another place in order to join him. The camp was rich in artists, academics and teachers. Central, which lacked the quadrangle-like effect of the sunken garden of Hutchinson Square, had a much higher number of musicians, rivalling Onchan.

The first intake at Onchan had been liberally sprinkled with professional artists, some of whom did notable work in the camp's magazine. These men, the professors, the students, the musicians and the artists were able to adapt to camp life. The rest could volunteer and go to classes, but they needed work to do and needed it badly.

Then, partly through the guidance and help of welfare workers and partly through their own initiative, the men's camps developed an exchange system somewhat similar to that which had been launched in Port Erin. A remarkable variety of trades and crafts were started for the mutual benefit. Men cobbled and made shoes; they tailored, they started hairdressing, they did leatherwork, carpentry, book-binding, furniture-making; they baked bread, they mended watches, and in most camps there were some very fine cooks, professional or amateur.

The camps were, of course, wired-in compounds mostly made up of boarding-houses and occasionally hotels. Like fish in bowls, the inmates could be seen from outside but had no escape except indoors. It was simple for the commander to set up an internal system giving the internees a lot of responsibility for the day-by-day running of the camp. New entrants were soon sorted out; Jews requiring Kosher food were given their own house or houses and would cook in their own manner; Nazi sympathizers had their own place. Each house elected its leader, who would be required to draw up a schedule of duties—cleaning, postal collection and cooking. Men in a group of houses would in turn elect a street leader. There would then be the camp leader, who would have access to the office for complaints, who would take orders

Seaside boundary of the Mooragh Camp, Ramsey, the first of the internment camps on the Isle of Man in the Second World War. The camp went back from the sea front and was sectioned off internally to prevent different nationals from intermingling. The pictures were taken shortly after a Finn was found stabbed to death on the pavement in the foreground (*above*)

The Loch Promenade, Douglas, showing private hotels which formed part of the Metropole Camp, with the barbed wire along the front

Part of the front at Douglas. The Falcon Cliff Hotel, at the top of the cliff, became the main hospital for the 1939–45 internment camps

Internees returning to camp under escort after their exercise from – probably – Onchan Camp outside Douglas

Coupon money used in the internment camps

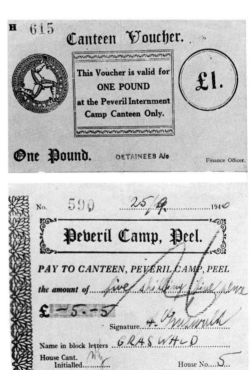

The captors (*above*) the later Chief Inspector S.M. Ogden, in charge of Peveril Camp, 1941–2, and (*right*) C.R.M. Cuthbert, Commandant at Port Erin and Port St Mary . . .

. . . and the captives (*below*): Professor Gerhard Bersu, the eminent archaeologist with a local farmer, and (*on right*) the artist Fred Uhlman, portrayed by fellow prisoner Kurt Schwitters, the Dadaist painter

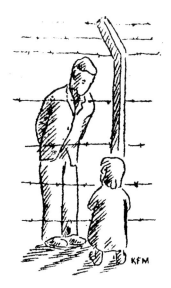

GREETINGS
Christmas 1940

Onchan's first internees produced
Christmas and Chanukah cards for
sending home or selling locally

WHAT WE ALL WISH
Victory
Peace
Home-Coming

GREETINGS
Christmas 1940

THE ONCHAN PIONEER

ERINNERUNGEN
Kempton Park - Drehkreuze

So mued sind viele und so tief verhaermt,
Dass sie nicht fuehlen, wie die Sonne waermt;

Und Blumen, die an ihren Wegen stoh'n,
Sind ihnen nichts, den Mueden, die nicht geh'n,

Dass noch ein Groesserer am Drehkreuz steht
Und prueft, wer diesen Weg der Leiden geht.

Dr. A.L. Oppenheimer

The German artists in the Hutchinson Camp produced sophisticated work from a duplicator. (*Above*) 'Three at Euston Station' by W. Schmeidler, showing two young women awaiting the arrival of the train from the north; Christmas Issue, 1941 (from the Collection of Mr Hilary Guard). (*Left*) page from the *Onchan Pioneer*, 5 January 1941

Royal Avenue, Onchan, as seen from the front page of the *Onchan Pioneer* in December 1940, and some years later

and make requests on behalf of the inmates. The leader, after consultation with his street or house leaders, would be expected to put forward names of men who wanted transfers, who wanted repatriation if it were ever possible, applications for release, enlistment in the forces and so on. The system had worked in the temporary camps on the mainland; it would work on the Isle of Man. It did.

Inevitably it produced friction, not always of a minor nature. Some camp commanders saw everything in military terms, and to them the leader was known as Camp Captain. A military-sounding title was unacceptable to the intellectuals of Hutchinson, who insisted on using Camp Leader or even Camp Father as the name. But however he was known, he could be useful to the other inmates and to the authorities.

It was the task of individual house captains to go to the camp's store at ten o'clock every morning and draw the rations that would be weighed out, taken back to the house and handed to the cook. At one time a wave of complaints, considered frivolous by officers in command, went through the camps alleging that internees were getting short weight. The moan was silenced by appointing the camp leader as referee. It became his duty to watch the morning hand-out and see that it was in order.

The day-by-day routine of the camps varied very little. Reveille was sounded at 7 a.m. at most places. After roll call and physical exercises, breakfast would be taken communally in camps such as Metropole, where there were hotels with suffi-cient dining-room accommodation; in the separate houses otherwise. There would be regular parades for escorted walks out of the barbed wire and along the Douglas front. In summer there would be more physical jerks on the beach and swimming in the sea. The day would otherwise be filled by educational classes and the increasing activities being organized by welfare officers.

At five in the evening the names would be announced of internees who were being released the following morning. This was a critical moment; release was the one word that mattered. Then, when the right name did not appear, there was depres-sion, lasting into the night and easing slowly as a little hope gathered strength the following day, only to be dashed again at a few minutes past five.

One of the first published reports on life inside the camps was given by Dr G. K. A. Bell, Bishop of Chichester, in a speech in the House of Lords early in August 1940. He had just returned from spending four days on the Isle of Man.

He alleged that there were 10,000 men, women and children in the Manx camps, a figure that was somewhat on the low side. He added that there were 2,800 German and Austrian internees at Huyton, near Liverpool.

The Bishop then stated that there were 1,900 internees in Central Camp in Douglas, and that of them 150 had been in Nazi concentration camps. Some of Hitler's leading political antagonists were interned, he alleged, and 'multitudes' of men on Hitler's black list were to be found in Huyton or on the Isle of Man. He urged that men with such backgrounds should be released speedily. 'In the Isle of Man and at Huyton,' he said, 'I was astounded at the quantity as well as the quality of the material available—doctors, professors, scientists, inventors, chemists, industrialists, manufacturers, humanists—they all want to work for Britain, freedom and justice.'

The speech was widely reported. It increased the growing feeling that the camps contained a gross wastage of valuable human material. At the same time serious newspapers were reporting a man released from the Isle of Man as saying that he had been a prisoner in Dachau and then, for four months, in Buchenwald. The Manx camps, he said, were 'Paradise' compared with the German. 'In Germany they would give twenty lashes for almost any minor offence.' By contrast, he claimed that at Douglas internees were shown every consideration. He also maintained that, while there had been no real medical facilities at Dachau, no one could have had better medical attention than was to be had on the island. All the aliens, he maintained, had been impressed by the good treatment they had received, and many of them were only too anxious to get out and serve in the British Army.

The cynic could question such interviews; a man could give them hoping to use them to his own advantage. The truth about conditions, once the first stampede was over, was that on the island they were as good as war allowed. Yet the allegations that Jews and anti-Nazis who had suffered in German concentration camps were later interned in Britain through inefficient screening is accurate enough, vouched for time and time again.

Morale among the internees improved enormously in August 1940. For the first time since internment reached the island, husbands in the Douglas camps were to meet their wives from Port Erin and Port St Mary. Two hundred women were to come to Douglas for a rendezvous at the Derby Castle, a vast entertainment centre that had been the pioneer of the huge dancehalls built in holiday towns all over Britain. The news created immediate excitement, even among those not involved; maybe it was a sign of better times ahead.

The wives were doubly elated, for many had recently had the immense consolation of receiving their children from the mainland. Youngsters who had been left behind in the first bewildering chaos of sudden internment were now being brought over in parties by the welfare organizations.

Preparations for the visit went ahead fervently in Port Erin. The Exchange Scheme's beauty parlour worked overtime. The hairdressers were heavily booked. Rushed work came in for the dressmakers and the improvised millinery workshop.

The meeting took place on the last Wednesday of August 1940, and the *Isle of Man Times* could not be blamed for finding the occasion heart-rending. The women had travelled to Douglas by train and then been taken on by coach. They were in a state of high excitement; in some cases this was to be the first meeting for months. The men had marched to the venue from their camps, some units with a guard of half a dozen soldiers with sidearms. The newspaper writer was not slow to record the eager look in the men's faces and the sad attempts that had been made to bring their women some token of affection. Hydrangea and fuchsia blooms had been taken from the gardens of the camp houses to be presented apologetically as bouquets.

The men were marshalled into sections on the dance floor and in the galleries; the women were late, and it was not until nearly four o'clock that they arrived. They too had brought small gifts. Report said that they had been orderly enough on arrival at the Castle, but when they suddenly saw their menfolk, they rushed forward to clutch and be clutched. For more than an hour they sat and talked in couples, catching up on all the things that had happened since their separation; talking of children, of whom the man might be getting reassuring news; talking of relatives; talking of home; talking of themselves and their problems.

The man from the *Isle of Man Times* did not fail to report on the fine, healthy appearance of both men and women; internment plainly was doing them no harm.

He found the parting even more heart-rending than the meeting. Most of the women kept up bravely but some wept openly and unashamedly. After the women had gone, the men marched back to their camps, but, we are assured, the spring had gone out of their step.

Thus ended one of the strangest reunion parties of the war, two hundred married couples, held virtual prisoner a few miles apart from each other, not knowing when they would be released back to their homes or even whether they would be released at all; not knowing if and when they would see each other again.

However, the party set a precedent. It was pronounced a success by the watchful authorities. It would be repeated at monthly intervals, in future to be held over in Port Erin, in what was and still is known as Collinson's Café, used throughout the life of the Rushen Camp as the women's recreational centre. And repeated it was, to the general content, even after the nature of the Port Erin Camp changed the following year.

In what would normally have been the end of the holiday season there came another announcement that was to help the men's morale. Internees were now to be permitted to work on the land. Applications for their services were to be made by the Manx farmers to the commander of the nearest camp.

This was the first sign of organized work for the men outside the camps and had been advocated for months by the welfare authorities. Paid labour for prisoners had always been a tricky matter, opposed by trade unions for many years throughout peace and war—traditionally they suspected it as a threat, undercutting established labour. It must be kept out altogether or maintained at the barest minimum. For generations prisoners in British gaols had been allowed to do little but the spiritless work of stitching mailbags.

Local farm work, however, was different. A harvest of sorts would soon be on its way, and it would need to be gathered in. So regulations were posted in the newspapers; farmers must employ groups of not less than twenty internees at a time, paying the camp commander a shilling a day for each of them, to be credited to the internee accordingly. The rate was later increased. The farmer would also pay the cost of transport where necessary. Internees would leave camp at 8.30 a.m., return at 5.30 and have an hour for a midday meal which would be provided by the farmer. There was one over-riding condition: internee labour had to be additional to the normal labour employed on the farm, not a substitute for it.

Landwork meant getting out; a change of scene; days away from a crowded and depressing camp. Fit men, excluding those now training for the Pioneer Corps enlistment and those pre-occupied with the increasing enterprises inside the camp, volunteered readily. There were pro-Nazis who refused to have anything to do with the scheme, on the grounds that helping to produce food was helping the British war effort, but in the main it worked well, and the outdoor work parties became part of the island scene for the rest of the war. The conditions were soon modified; it ceased to be necessary for the men to be employed in groups of twenty. Farmers could soon apply for any number they wanted; the camps would provide escort and guard, picking up and dropping men off at the farms as required.

One of the first men to volunteer for farm work from Metropole Camp was Giovanni Maneta. Work on the land meant a change of routine, the sound of the country instead of the clatter of the Douglas promenade, the chance to hear a voice that was not an internee's or a guard's. In Maneta's experience the Manx farmers treated their new-found labour very well. They were glad of the help and the men sat at table for the midday meal like one large family, a familiarity that camp authorities tried to stop for a time as it amounted to fraternizing. In this they failed. Maneta was lucky once more. He was taken right down to the southern end of the island, to a farm that was just off the coastal road linking Castletown with Port St Mary and Port Erin. He remembers it now with affection, particularly its apple pie, a dish which was a rarity for an Italian seaman.

As autumn approached, the impact of the war machine was felt increasingly in the Isle of Man. New regulations kept appearing. Coal, always more expensive than on the mainland, was scarce, and the ancient Manx right to cut peat on the island's central spine was applied for more and more. Peat provided work and exercise and winter heat.

More than 3,000 Manxmen had registered for military service. Tea was now rationed at two ounces a week, giving cause for much grumbling. The four-ounce butter ration did not greatly worry the Manx, for it seemed that everyone knew a farmer who had milk to spare and knew how to make use of it. More and more the tramp of the troops was loud in the land, and using this tag as an advertising slogan an enterprising trader in Douglas urged his readers not to let them tramp over good carpets but to buy and lay his linoleum.

Compensation was announced to boarding-house keepers whose premises had been requisitioned. The terms were fair but hardly generous. Broadly, when a house had been commandeered, the contents left behind were valued by an assessor appointed by the Manx Government. A percentage of the value was then paid as a yearly rent. It started at fifteen per cent for the first £100 and went down to 7½ per cent on any value over £1,000. There was also a five per cent rent on all hot and cold water installations at cost. The annual rent would then be paid by four quarterly instalments. A landlady who felt aggrieved could appeal against the valuation.

The Manx Press greeted the compensation terms cautiously, agreeing that they probably favoured the small householder.

Inevitably, nobody was quite satisfied. There was more grumbling. The grouse was well established as the avian symbol of war. It was understandable, for as the September of 1940 advanced, more and more property was taken into the temporary custody of the internment camp administration or the armed forces. The latest area to be commandeered was a prime site in the centre of the Loch Promenade, Douglas, consisting of two blocks of large boarding-houses, in addition to the Sefton, which was one of the best hotels in the town, and the Gaiety Theatre. Away in Peel the camp area was extended, and house-owners on the coast road to Ramsey were ordered out.

There was yet another change in public attitude, not against internees as such, but against the enemy, with the bombing of London and the North, as well as the Battle of Britain, which had hardened opinion. Anti-German feeling was running high.

German and Italian internees had arranged to give a concert in Douglas for the funds of Noble's Hospital. There was a wealth of musical talent in the camps, inside which concerts were held regularly. This outside effort in aid of the island's main hospital was backed by the hospital's committee; with the promise of patronage from the Lieutenant-Governor, there was a ready demand for tickets.

Then soon, as the air war intensified, there came growing opposition. Letters protesting against the concert appeared in the Manx newspapers, and even on the mainland. There were rumours of threatened demonstrations.

The event was cancelled. It was a sign of the times.

During the autumn two items emerged to increase such optimism as the internees managed to preserve, however difficult the circumstances.

It was suddenly announced that the far-away wives of the men in the camps could apply for permits to visit their husbands. This pleased both internees and seaside landladies. To the latter, hard pressed by the loss of their holiday trade, it meant customers from the mainland, not free-spending ones perhaps, but customers all the same.

The women came over steadily, causing the police to increase their vigilance against letter-smuggling from the camps. Too many wives were prepared to act as couriers, and a number of prosecutions followed as departing visitors and the occasional woman released from Rushen were found to be carrying uncensored mail intended for posting on the mainland. Often such letters were strongly pro-Nazi. The prosecution was automatic, and the sentence was usually two months' imprisonment.

Such cases were but a small minority. The decision to allow the visits continued throughout the war.

On 16 September 1940 C. R. M. Cuthbert, Divisional Detective Inspector in the Metropolitan Police, arrived in Douglas and signed in at the modest Ridgeway Hotel conveniently situated near Police Headquarters and the Administrative Offices of the internment camps. Mr Cuthbert was a quiet man who avoided the limelight and detested publicity, an attitude which stayed with him even into his retirement. His arrival went unreported in the Manx newspapers. Had they known that the man widely regarded as the pioneer of scientific forensic work was visiting Douglas, they would have become very excited. In fact the

Inspector had no thoughts of police work on his mind. He had for some months been concentrating on the examination of aliens by tribunal and had become an authority on that highly specialized subject.

He had not been on the island ten days when it was announced that a tribunal was to be set up at the Douglas Court House to consider cases for the release, where appropriate, of internees in the B category. It was known to the authorities as the B Advisory Committee.

It was soon learned that Monday 7 October would see the tribunal's first hearing, and the Manx newspapers went so far as to say that, while the names of those comprising the tribunal were to be kept secret, a Scotland Yard officer would represent the Government side. It was also known that applications of women aliens would be taken first and that the tribunal would sit for a fortnight, meeting daily, and possibly longer.

First news of all this had come on 24 September, 1940, when a Home Office advisory committee met at St Andrew's Hall in Douglas and notified the Manx authorities that a tribunal to consider release applications would be set up. In practice there was not one tribunal on the island but two. A special 'court' was separately set up to take the Italian cases, under Sir Percy Lorraine, who had been British Ambassador in Rome; it sat in Douglas.

In the camps the reaction was immediate. Internees, easily excitable at their plight, saw the possibility of the gates opening. Releases might now become general, instead of being so very slow. To get out: that was the problem. It was a matter for more and more letter-writing: to the welfare organizations in Bloomsbury House, to Members of Parliament, to solicitors, bank managers, ex-employers, or even to characters of national distinction who were unknown to the letter-writer but who were held to be men of compassion. To get out at all costs.

According to the Manx records, thirty-one women were taken under escort from Rushen to Douglas for the opening hearing. The daily entry then varied little; the file of applicants was long, the process was painstaking. The fact that nearly thirty cases could be considered in one session shows that no time was wasted.

The hearings did not last a fortnight, as had been predicted. They went on steadily until July 1941, when they were concentrated on St Andrew's Hall. There they continued. The last entry is for 8 September 1941, a full eleven months after the start. By then the internment scene had changed dramatically.

8

The Medical Back-Up

A substantial and well-organized medical back-up was needed for an internee population rising hurriedly to about 14,000 and then declining over the years until it was merely a matter of hundreds. In this the doctors and dentists and the hospitals of the Isle of Man played an important part. There were more than thirty doctors in practice on the island when the camps were opened. The number is imprecise as some men had already gone into the services, and their deputies were not necessarily permanent; in other cases practices had to be pooled hurriedly as a man joined the forces. However, at least seventeen local doctors had direct dealings with the internees.

The system, which evolved quickly and worked very efficiently, was simple: internee medical matters in the men's camps were ultimately the responsibility of the military, who in turn recruited local general practitioners to look after the individual camps.

From the start there was always a Royal Army Medical Corps presence in the island supervising that side of internment camp life. At first it was small, but it grew steadily, established to the central camp administration behind the seafront at Douglas. The day-to-day medical work was carried out mainly by the local doctors, in some cases helped by a doctor who was himself an internee.

The Manx practitioners were invited to undertake this work by the Government Secretary, who made the selection and informed the Manx Camps Division. The work was additional to the doctor's normal duties, and how he organized it was up to him entirely. The usual procedure was for the doctor to take his private morning surgery from, say, nine to ten, and then proceed straight to his camp, where his work would depend on the daily number of cases. For this he would be paid £1 a day. As in the early days of 1941 he might easily have had the care of two thousand or more anxious and worried men behind the wires, it seems an extremely modest fee. Yet it was really not unreasonable. In those times a general practitioner would not expect more than a few shillings for a short consultation and would be prepared to be called out for perhaps 7s. 6d. (37½p.). Even the lordly ones of distant Harley Street were ready to give a full hour of their expert time for 3 guineas (£3. 15p.). So £1 a day for an extra responsibility was not to be argued about.

Each camp had its own small medical unit or sick-bay, some larger than others. Here the local doctor would see his patients and keep his camp records. The unit would deal with the common ailments and with first-aid cases. A bed patient who could not be looked after in the sick-bay would be sent on to one of the island hospitals at the doctor's discretion according to his complaint and condition.

The small medical unit might have an orderly who would probably work on a rota system and who would be an internee. He would be paid at the very modest rate given for camp work. Dispensing would be handled by an RAMC dispenser.

There were many medical men among the internees, particularly in the early stages. Such men could be used, again at the discretion of the Manx doctor in charge, and almost all of them spoke excellent English. One would be selected as the liaison man who would telephone the doctor in any emergency. There was no shortage of volunteers. The number of internee doctors declined rapidly in the shifting camp population; they were more valuable outside. All the same, a few men, who if not pro-Nazi were at least strongly pro-German, remained behind the wire right through the war. They were a considerable help; officially they could recommend prescriptions and even treatment, but they could not order them. The wise doctor was glad to have their services.

Some of the camps had medical units that seemed to develop

an identity of their own. Hutchinson, in the centre of Douglas, used Arrandale, one of its houses, as a sick-bay; Metropole fitted out the Dodsworth boarding-house for the same purpose. Onchan and Mooragh improvised small medical units in their own grounds, using outbuildings. The main camps in the built-up area of Douglas had to put such units into houses, sometimes occupying only a room or two where space was precious.

Central, the first of the really crowded camps, was a typical case. The Manx doctor was provided with a rudimentary surgery on the ground floor of a house at the foot of Castle Drive, almost opposite the entrance to the Castle Mona Hotel. It was convenient for the camp offices which were in the shops on the front below the hotel, and it was well situated for seeing patients. Within a week of its opening, the camp population had risen to 2,906, from which it steadily receded. It was never as overcrowded as Palace, which followed it a week later and which shortly after it opened was crammed with just over 2,900 men, but it had one quite extraordinary feature. It contained nearly 200 Jewish doctors, almost none of whom was a general practitioner; nearly every man had full consultant status. Those who were surgeons had arrived with cases of valuable instruments. Some were highly specialized and very eminent men indeed, a deplorable waste of talent. Inevitably they were in the main released speedily, but while they were there, the Manx physician who made his daily visit to the camp was in a unique position. If he wanted to have a second opinion, he could whistle up and take his pick immediately from any of two hundred. It was an opportunity not to be missed.

The Douglas general practitioner was a wise man. He organized a simple system whereby every internee in the camp was examined by a specialist. He would then receive a report. Where it was desirable for him to check he would do so; where he agreed there was a long-term problem, he would recommend release on compassionate grounds. He could only recommend, but he had influence. Tribunals gave such claims priority.

The medical internees who formed such a remarkable corps in the Central Camp had been collected mainly in London, where most of them were working for higher degrees in the postgraduate medical schools. Their religion gave them a strong bond, stronger probably in adversity than in ordinary everyday life, and they held their Jewish services in the ballroom of the Lido, a large dance-hall only a few yards along the front from the camp. The Manx practitioner who looked after them still recalls how the Jewish consultants invited him to one of their services, at which internees would recite their verses in English. He went hatted and remained impressed, sensing the way their religion linked them even more deeply together in their plight.

In a smaller way the Italians at Granville Camp, also on the promenade but a way to the south, had their own corps of medical men. The same doctor, now living in retirement in the island, was transferred to look after the health side of Granville when it opened nearly five months later. There he met Paul E. Polani, who had come to London from Trieste a year before the war, having started what was to become a brilliant career as a geneticist, later rising to be Emeritus Professor of Paediatric Research in the University of London. He was the man picked by the Manx MO to assist him, and he in turn was assisted by Dr B. L. della Vida, who later specialized in chemical pathology in Italy. It was men like these who were the subject of the outside protests that so much talent was being wasted behind barbed wire.

A very different case was that of the Rushen Camp at Port Erin and Port St Mary, which had an ambitious medical back-up. Part of the Hydro Hotel, a large building on the Port Erin seafront, which soon became camp HQ, was used as a sick-bay for the women of the two camps, and later also as the medical centre for the Married Camp as well. Rushen came under the Home Office for administration purposes and not the military, and Doctor Margaret Colls, a Home Office doctor, arrived from London almost at the start and took charge. She remained at Port Erin throughout the war. Local doctors and dentists visited daily. Nursing in the camp was under the control of four district nursing officers, all attached to the camp staff, who were State Registered nurses. An English nursing sister and nurses looked after the camp hospital in the Hydro. There was, of course, a wealth of nursing talent among the internees, but the Lutheran sisters from the German Hospital in London mostly received what was known as 'the German Money' and therefore would not have helped in that way.

Peveril at Peel was like Port Erin in that it had more ambitious medical arrangements than the rest. But Peveril, being a camp with a high proportion of detainees, came directly under RAMC supervision with a senior officer, usually Lieutenant-Colonel R. Flowerdew, in charge of Ballaquane, the camp's hospital unit. Routine medical matters were taken by a local doctor, who had an internee doctor to help him. The building was directly behind the main camp; before the war it had been a guest-house for youth organizations. It had a population of patients and staff which varied week by week up to around fifty.

All the men's camps had a central hospital to which cases could be transferred where necessary. This was Falcon Cliff Hospital, sited at the commandeered Falcon Cliff Hotel on the steep rise behind Douglas promenade. This too came under military administration, sometimes involving Lieutenant-Colonel Flowerdew, sometimes Colonel Barker, who had spent most of his working life in India. It was a joke among the medical fraternity on the island that after his arrival the incidence of malaria seemed noticeably to have increased, judging by the amount of quinine on prescription.

Falcon Cliff was small but highly organized and even ran a specialized out-patients clinic for internees. The whole unit was roughly the size of Ballaquane at Peel with up to about fifty patients and staff. An internee doctor, who rose to a position of eminence in London after the war, was appointed to the hospital, whose head man was always RAMC. The orderlies were Army men, usually of poor medical rating themselves. Surprisingly the matron and nurse were civilians from the mainland.

Falcon Cliff was not for acute or long-term patients who might require specialized treatment. For such cases the camp authorities could call on the island's main and generously endowed medical services. Noble's, named after Henry Bloom Noble, the philanthropist who died early in the century and who created it, was and remains the senior Manx hospital, where the island's pathology and such are centralized. Surgical and long-treatment medical cases were moved there regularly from the camps. It was a rule that when women internees were admitted from Rushen they would always be screened off when put in general women's wards. Maternity cases from Port Erin and Port St Mary were also sent to hospital in Douglas.

The island's isolation hospital was White Hoe, a short distance outside Douglas town. It took suspected fever cases and such conditions as polio which were far too prevalent in those days, and the internment camps produced their quota of patients. The physician in charge of it, who had been on the island for more than ten years and had a general practice on the Loch Promenade, Douglas, had been the first medical appointment to a camp when he was invited to look after Central.

Suspected tuberculosis cases were sent up under escort for investigation to the Cronk Ruagh sanatorium outside Ramsey in the north, where they came under a physician who practised in the town and where they would be admitted as in-patients if necessary.

The internment camps put their greatest strain on Braddan Mental Hospital, Ballamona, the island's only unit of its type. The average number of patients admitted there had been fifty a year over the seventy-five years of its pre-war history. Now, suddenly, admissions were running at 107 a year, most of the increase being due to the internees. Such were the statistics of anxiety and frustration.

The number of patients on the Ballamona register—including out-patients having treatment—had increased to more than 300 by the end of 1941, and at one time the camp authorities attached an NCO and three soldiers to the hospital to look after internees who were patients. The figures then declined steadily as the releases started and the camps thinned out.

When the last one closed, early in September 1945, months after the war was over, eight internee patients were left behind in Ballamona.

One thing can be said confidently about the internees on the island: they were very healthy. They had a well-balanced diet; they could take plenty of outdoor exercise if they wished and were fit for it; their living-conditions were in the main very satisfactory apart from some overcrowding in the early days; they had adequate warmth and clothing; their medical support was well organized and very thorough. Their enemy was anxiety, and with some it could be a serious foe indeed, despite efforts by the authorities to find work for idle and worried hands. Even so, some people in the camps were deeply wretched, full of frustration and bitterness, and there were suicides, particularly in the early days.

However, in the first two years of the women's camps the total number of deaths from any reason was only ten—in a camp population that at one time approached 4,000. It was a statistic of which authority had no need to be ashamed. It compared favourably with the natural death rate in the civil population.

9

New Year In

On the last day of 1940 there were 3,136 women in the Rushen camps, most of them in Port Erin. The figures always varied from day to day; there would be intakes, transfers and releases. But the overall figure was falling steadily. It was the same story in the men's camps. In these, at the end of the year, the number of internees was down to 6,900. In addition, there were fourteen 'special' internees in two houses outside the camps. The 'specials'—so listed at the time—are believed to have been German consular officials who could not get back to their own country.

The total of just over 10,000 at the end of the traumatic year of 1940 is about 4,000 below the figure five months earlier. Larger estimates of the internee population have been given from time to time, but can be discounted. By the winter of 1940–41 the work of the tribunals was showing through.

The Manx had been spared the air battles and the nightly raids but they had read of the pounding of London and the south-east and they were angry, like the rest of the country; they read of Coventry and they were horrified. They were well aware of the enemy flying steadily deeper into Britain. They heard the drone of bombers on missions to Belfast and Glasgow. Sometimes they heard the thud as bombs were jettisoned. Increasingly the southern night sky would glow with the fires started in Liverpool and the Mersey shipping basin; as far as the Manx were concerned, the serious bombing of Liverpool had started on 27 September, when the Steam Packet Company's sailing-sheet stated in red ink: 'Liverpool Coburg Dock bombed. 35 tons Ramsey cargo destroyed by fire and water.' A month later, in the last days of October, the attack on Liverpool intensified. The port was closed to the Manx ships for lengthy periods; on Friday 25 October no steamer left Douglas for the mainland port, one of the rarest events in more than a hundred years' operation of the line. Two days later the company's shed on No. 5 Dock at Liverpool was directly hit. There was loss of life, much damage and much loss of cargo. Two Manx cargo vessels that were in port escaped the full blast but were damaged by falling debris.

The raids continued and became even more severe in December. The city and docks were heavily bombed in the week before Christmas. By the Saturday all sailings were cancelled from the Isle of Man, and the vital port of Liverpool was closed to the islanders. It remained closed on Sunday and late into Monday morning. On Christmas Eve the Steam Packet, for generations the Manx lifeline, switched its sailing plans and took nearly 300 passengers to Fleetwood. On 27 December the *Victoria* was mined about eight miles out from Liverpool when homeward bound with about 200 passengers. They were saved, and so was the steamer, which was towed ashore and later returned to war service. But enough was enough; at the year's end the Steam Packet directors took the key decision. Henceforth Fleetwood was their mainland port, and so it remained until 1946.

On the Isle of Man itself the year ended on a subdued note. The internees led their aimless lives, longing for release; the services went about their business guarding, training and watching; the Manx helped where they were encouraged, giving talks to troops and internees in turn when it was considered suitable, waiting with tea and cake at the monthly meetings between internees and their wives, or at the socials arranged in all parts of the island between the local people and the visiting servicemen.

It was revealed that 800 children from the mainland were now evacuated to the island and attending school. The Manx women were pleased at the news, for back in October they had been told there were only 640.

Yet in all the circumstances it was not a bad Christmas. The local Press carried columns of advertisements for seasonal titbits. The Manx were always cheerful trenchermen; they produced first-class meat and they liked to eat it, just as they knew how to deal with their famous kipper. 'The best and nothing but the best this Christmas,' proclaimed one leading butcher. 'Choice selection of home fed turkeys, geese, ducks and chickens. Prime home fed heifer beef, wether mutton and pork. Special sausages.' It made robust reading. At the other end of the crossing it would have startled Liverpudlians, whose food markets were dislocated by the bombings.

Indeed, it would have startled most people on the mainland, for the public's meat ration was falling steadily and at the start of January 1941 the official allowance was only meat to the value of 1s. 10d. (9p.) a week, which, even allowing for the general fall in the value of money over the last forty-odd years, is surely derisory. It was not a ration to satisfy the ardent carnivore, and within a few more months it was to drop to its lowest point throughout the entire war.

Meanwhile, in the internment camps the men consoled themselves with one vital statistic. Three out of every ten who had been behind the wire in August had since been released. More than a quarter. It justified that strange word: hope.

10

Trouble with the Ladies

Dame Joanna Cruickshank had little time for the niceties of public relations; only once, during her year as Commandant at the Rushen Camp, did she lead over the parapet, look down at the ground and talk to the old *Manchester Guardian*. Not for nothing had she done her training at Guy's Hospital all those years ago; she was ever a nurse, and she was indeed a very grand one. The camps, she reported with enthusiasm, had a 'wonderful' health record. Many of the women had arrived as chronic cases, but there had been a great improvement in general health. Children who had been poorly when they reached the island, many of them suffering from malnutrition, were now 'bursting with health and happiness'. One would not see bonnier children anywhere.

Both camps, Port Erin and Port St Mary, she explained, had a health superintendent who was assisted by internee doctors and nurses. There was a clinic for adults and another for the children, and in six months there had been only one death—a bad heart case.

'Our own people,' said Dame Joanna, 'would have to pay a high price for the treatment the camp's maternity cases were receiving.'

She explained how a large number of children lived happily with their mothers, but although living under internment conditions the youngsters themselves were not internees. The younger ones attended two schools which had highly trained teachers. Interned women science students could receive permits to work in the Marine Biological Station at Port Erin, and chief among them was a qualified scientist who did first-class research work there for Manchester University while on the island. The Station was also open to children and internees for lectures and a study of the exhibits.

Turning from health care and child welfare, Dame Joanna reported glowingly on the various occupations arranged for the internees including lessons in languages, of which the English classes were by far the most popular. She emphasized that there were also experts who gave lessons in the domestic sciences. A talented Austrian sculptor gave clay-modelling classes, and her pupils were doing good work. With the help of the internees themselves, the Commandant said, she had organized an inter-change of services between the women, and she went on to explain the scheme described later by Ruth Borchardt. Certainly Dame Joanna had been far-sighted enough to give it her official blessing and had provided as much direct aid as she could. She explained how clothes and materials sent to the island were remodelled or made up. The women, she added, knitted for the men in the camps across the island, who in return took on the cobbling and such jobs.

There had been personal quarrels between the Nazi women and some of the others, Dame Joanna admitted, but they had not been serious. In six months there had never been any real trouble. Women listed as Nazis were put into quarters by themselves, and the Jewesses had theirs.

The Commandant then revealed that the British Government was considering setting up a camp for married internees. It was the first public disclosure of this development. Meanwhile, she said, wives were meeting their husbands once a month and could talk for two hours.

'The authorities are doing their best,' concluded Dame Joanna. They had no desire to keep anyone on the island unnecessarily, and there were very few restrictions for the women, who were free to go anywhere in the wide area where the camps were situated. They could shop, go to the cinema and attend the church of their own denomination. They were 'free of the beaches and many enjoyed bathing'.

Dame Joanna herself was to be 'free of the beaches' before

many months were out, although in her case there was no
question of bathing from the Isle of Man.

The disclosure that a camp was likely to be set up for married
couples caused alarm among the Manx landladies of Port St
Mary. They assumed—rightly as it turned out—that as and when
such a camp was created, it would be housed in their village
rather than in neighbouring Port Erin, where there was the main
concentration of women internees.

Many of the landladies were spinsters or widows; they were
perfectly happy to have women, even foreign women, billeted on
them. This meant that some income would be coming in, however modest. But a man about the house and a foreign one at that;
this was alarming; 109 women promptly signed a petition protesting most strongly against any such development. It went on
its way, getting nowhere.

There was as yet no official confirmation of the setting-up of
the married camp, but news and nonsense travel at speed behind
barbed wire.

The steadily mounting number of releases and this new story
about a mixed camp certainly delighted the women internees of
Port Erin; it made wildly exciting speculation for those sadly short
but ecstatic minutes with husbands once a month.

However, not all the women internees had husbands on the
islands, and perhaps only a few could hope to join their men in
internment. What would be the basis for selection? Here was a
new worry, an excuse for anxiety once more. So, however hopeful the signs—and they were increasingly hopeful—depression
remained the greatest single curse of the camps, male or female.
January was not out when the first suicide of 1941 went into the
files at Port Erin. She was a forty-eight-year-old German
internee, and her body was found on the rocks below the lifeboat
station. She was reported as having been suffering from depression.

She was not the only one.

Early in February senior officials of the Home Office made a
brief trip to the Isle of Man. The rumour was to become a fact;
there was to be a married camp. On 10 February 1941 Dame
Joanna convened a meeting to sort out arrangements. Of one
thing she was very sure: extra personnel would be needed.

This might seem a statement of the obvious, but to the Manx
police it was a serious matter. They were extended as never

extended before, working six days a week often for very long hours, attending to a vast number of extra duties due to the war and the presence of the internment camps. At least the men's camps did not need guarding around their perimeter by the police, but there were no soldiers at the women's camps so extra police watch was needed, and a new camp for married internees would be another headache. Manpower was desperately short in wartime, and in a specialized area like the Isle of Man the job of a Chief Constable was placidly to achieve the impossible while performing a delicate balancing operation between the Lieutenant Governor, the Manx Government, the local administration, representatives of various distant Government departments and the local military, naval and RAF establishments, while at the same time maintaining law and order and helping generally in the administration of justice.

Major John William Young was the man for the task. He had spent his active career in the Indian Army and then the Bengal Police and had come to the island as Chief Constable in 1936. He was an able administrator and committee man, a heavy cigar-smoker who seemed to wave his argument in his hand as he made his contribution to discussion. Not only did he recognize a good letter when he saw it, he could usually write a better one himself, drafting it carefully in longhand. He is remembered today for the clarity of his memoranda and by some recipients for the brevity of his bluntness.

The Major was a distant figure to many of the men on the beat and an almost unknown one to some. Yet he was mindful that they were part of his duty, and they respected him. He left the day-to-day running of the force to his Superintendent and he kept a tidy desk; but he checked and cross-checked on all police affairs, and he automatically assumed complete personal command of all policy matters. He lived near Government House, and he had formed a close link with the Lieutenant Governor, Lord Granville, and with the very able Government Secretary, Bertram Sargeaunt, the most senior of the Manx civil servants. As the war developed, he moved easily among the army officers, so many of them recalled from the Retired List, who ran the camps. He was at home with the various military security officers.

To him fell the responsibility of deploying his meagre force, totalling about seventy-five men, so that they covered the new duties and handled the snowstorm of paper. Those were days when a policeman's life was certainly not a happy one, at least in terms of worldly goods. Men still in the service can recall how they joined as cadets and were paid £1. 5s. (£1. 25p.) a week, with 5¾d. (2½p.) an hour overtime, later raised to 6¼d. (approximately 3p.). Those attached to the CID often worked from nine in the morning until nine at night through a six-day week. The overtime was paid quarterly, when an exhausted young man might for once find himself with a few pounds in his pocket.

It became known inside the local civil service, which had an Internment Camps Division for administration purposes, that the new development would open from 1 April. It was decided that single women in Port St Mary, or wives who for some reason were not rejoining their husbands, would be transferred to Port Erin. The two camps would be separated. A neutral zone between them would be restored to the Manx.

The news came out publicly early in April after some delay; the new camp would not be ready until the end of the first week in May. And its Commandant was to be Divisional Detective Inspector C. R. M. Cuthbert of Scotland Yard, more recently installed at the tribunal in Douglas and now promoted to Chief Inspector. After long conferences between so many interested parties, it was agreed with the police that the married quarters would be confined to the Promenade at Port St Mary, that its fenced boundary would include only the houses on the front with the two fields behind them and that a control point would be placed where the Promenade joined the main road that led out of the village.

One of Mr Cuthbert's first actions after his appointment was announced was to hold a number of small, informal meetings with the people of Port St Mary. He sensed the alarm among the inhabitants. Steadily he convinced them that only men—and women—of proven good character would be admitted to the married camp. He circulated the men's camps emphasizing that transfer would be a real privilege. Any misbehaviour would result in the culprit's being sent back. This caution accounted for the small numbers joining the new camp that May: the figure increased after careful vetting. The people of Port St Mary were reassured.

To some Mr Cuthbert's appointment in charge of the married

camp must have come as a surprise. Dame Joanna would almost certainly have known of it in advance. It is hard to believe that she would have liked it, although she was well aware of the man's expert knowledge on internment matters, having consulted him frequently.

A Home Office official, Miss Joan D. Wilson, who was attached to the Prison Commission Service, was appointed his deputy with special responsibility for the women. She had come to the island from her position as Deputy Governor of Walton Prison, Liverpool. She was described as a very strong personality. She worked very successfully with the Commandant for a year, before returning to the Prison Service at Walton. After the war she went to Germany as Controller of Women's Penal Establishments under the Allied Military Government. Her replacement on the Isle of Man was Miss Mona R. J. Edwards.

Meanwhile the rules at the main women's camp at Port Erin had been sharpened up; internees were now barred from making purchases of more than 5s. a week without permission, which went some way to cancelling out the inequality between those who had money behind them and those with little or nothing. Shops were forbidden to give credit to internees, who were equally forbidden to ask for any. Sales of alcoholic drinks, electric light bulbs, torches, candles, spirit lamps and methylated spirits were banned. And in future any money sent to internees, or given or paid to them, must go through the camp bank.

Some might think that the surprising thing about these restrictions is that they were issued in mid-March 1941. It seems strange that they had not been in force since the arrival of the women on the island back in the previous summer. On the very day they were announced, a thirty-one-year-old German internee was missing from the Dandy Hill Hospital inside the Port Erin camp. She normally lived at the Golf Links Hotel, whose internees were almost entirely pro-Nazi. Her body was later found down among the rocks. She had left a note in German, and she was the second melancholy suicide in less than two months.

One group of internees took the news of the married camp with alarm. The single women at Port St Mary feared—rightly as it turned out—that they would be moved across to Port Erin to join the larger section of the Rushen Camp. This they did not want.

Perhaps because they had so little to which to attach their loyalty, so little with which to identify themselves with pride, the women internees considered that they divided sharply between the two villages in which they were billeted. The Port St Mary internees felt that they were in some way the senior set; they were the intellectuals; they had the superior team spirit; Port Erin merely held the hearties. It was absurd, maybe; it was certainly quite illogical, but both groups gave a sharp identity to their own set, like schoolboys strutting in the camaraderie of a real or imagined school house.

The day for which the internees had been waiting was now 8 May 1941. During the previous week there had been comings and goings among the women of the two villages. Internees were moving out from the one into the other. By the morning of the day when the married camp was officially opened there were 166 women internees waiting there for their menfolk; those women who were not involved in the new camp were now across in Port Erin.

By the end of the day 162 men had arrived from the Douglas camps. It was a start. By the end of June 1941 it held 162 males and 170 women, and by the end of the year 143 and 157. (The difference in the figures is explained by the admission of some internees on compassionate grounds.) On 19 August 1942, when it was transferred to Port Erin, where it remained until it was disbanded in October 1944, the camp population was 116 and 122, the release system having been busy.

Right from the start the married camp had its own educational and social programmes, later to be developed considerably after the move to the upper part of Port Erin. A small school was organized, and among its first teachers was Margaret Collyer, who had been one of Dame Joanna's original welfare helpers.

To the police the new camp provided its own problems; there were new control points to be manned, new boundaries to be watched. There were photographs to be taken of every male alien, and new parties to escort, new internment lists to be kept and a close liaison to be maintained with the camp administration.

Although she is no longer alive to put her own side in any argument, it must surely be reasonable to assume that Dame Joanna was unhappy when the married camp started. She was a distinguished woman in a highly specialized field; she was sixty-five; she had already seen active service in one major war, and in the next one she had agreed to be Commandant of the Rushen

Camp. Now she found a new camp, which she had helped to create at meeting after meeting, and she saw it working—and working under a man; a man with no knowledge of nursing. It was not *her* camp. It must have been hurtful.

Dame Joanna had not helped herself by her attitude to some important local officials. Major Young, Chief Constable of the island, had reason to complain of her habit of threatening to refer anything to which she objected to the Home Office in London. Alternatively, she would threaten to resign. She had been known to harangue her victim on long and high-pitched telephone calls. And she had assured the head of the Manx police that she knew more about security than he did, a remark with which he smoothly agreed at the time, but it was not likely to have been forgotten. He dismissed it all as being due to 'nerves'. The signalled arrival of five women internees escorted by four police-women made her suspect that she would be dealing with some new and dangerous customers, and the taciturn Major assumed she was becoming jumpy. The local opinion that difficulties of this sort would not arise in Port St Mary did not go unreported on high.

It may or may not have been a coincidence, but within a fortnight of the opening of the new camp Dame Joanna had resigned. Her departure was announced on 22 May. She was back in London the same day. Accompanying her to town was her deputy, Miss Elizabeth E. Looker, described as the scholarly warden of Edinburgh University's hostels for women students. She had chosen to go with her chief.

Miss Looker is remembered after more than forty years for one personal oddity—she spoke at the most extraordinary speed. 'Even faster than Patrick Moore,' attested one contemporary. The next in seniority was a Miss Bloom. Both women left with the Dame. Certainly there was resentment by some at the thought of a women's camp having a man as its Commandant. A question was even asked in Parliament.

The Home Office stated merely that Dame Joanna had 'asked to be allowed to relinquish her post', which she had held for one year. 'The Home Secretary has accepted the resignation of Dame Joanna and Miss Looker with the greatest regret,' an official told the newspapers. 'Their administration was most successful in the face of many difficulties'—which was a fair statement.

That same official announcement advised that Chief Inspector

Cuthbert was now appointed Commandant at both the Port Erin women's camp and the married camp. His deputy at Port St Mary, Miss Wilson, would now be second in command at both camps, again in special charge of the women's interests.

'Secrecy surrounds the resignation,' said a writer in the London *Evening Standard*. That Dame Joanna's administration had been successful could not be disputed. Aided by some dedicated assistants she had brought order out of chaos in the first place, and had then maintained it, treading on quite an assortment of important feet in the process.

Chief Inspector Cuthbert had moved from Douglas to the Ballaqueeney Hotel in Port St Mary; inside the married camp, when he opened it. Later he took a furnished house in St George's Crescent, Port Erin. He believed firmly that a camp commander must live inside his camp. He declined the house that had been requisitioned for Dame Joanna; it was some distance away.

11

A Collection of Characters

After what seemed to him a long, long wait, Dr Hermann Scholz was at last removed from Huyton Camp in Lancashire and was transferred to Onchan in the Isle of Man. He arrived there in the early spring of 1941 but did not stay many months, for Onchan was run down and closed at the end of July. It stayed closed until September, when it reopened with Italian internees; its original Germans had mainly been released, and those that were still interned were transferred to Hutchinson, Scholz among them.

Once settled in Hutchinson, the young doctor continued his work as assistant to the Manx doctor who had daily responsibility for the medical side of the camp. Once again he was able to say that he was not helping the British war effort.

In Hutchinson he was one of the leading figures in some trouble that involved the integrity of an officer. He said later that it was he who laid the original allegations to authority, and he did it in a manner that avoided the official censorship. He contrived to write direct to Dr Huber, one of the Swiss delegation that acted as the protecting power for the Germans, and he alleged ill treatment and misbehaviour by the guard troops. A court of inquiry was ordered, and Scholz was one of the witnesses who had claimed that there were breaches of the Convention. Incidents revealed and arising from the inquiry led to the removal of the officer, who was found not guilty of the charges.

It was not long before Dr Scholz was also transferred. He was moved over to Metropole. To authority he must have been a complicated and most unusual internee, a man who did not fit easily into any of the categories. He was wholly German, very articulate and very anti-Nazi. Yet he was not Jewish and he was no political activist. He favoured Germany and made no effort to disguise the fact. He labelled himself, by his own statements, as a Class A internee. He was not a man to expect or to receive release. He was there for the duration. And as the man who had initiated the investigation at Hutchinson, he had marked his own card. It is easy enough to imagine what the NCOs in the office thought of him. He was a 'rum one', a character. There were many such.

At about this time the authorities were planning the development of the married camp at Port St Mary; the streamlining of the main men's camps in Douglas was proceeding steadily. From a total of roughly 7,000 male internees at the end of 1940, the figure had dropped to 5,300 by April 1941 and fallen again to less than 4,700 by the start of May, when it was significant that Peveril, the Peel camp, was empty. The intention was to fill it again, with a different breed of inmate.

The pattern of the releases was always the same. The previous evening a man whose discharge had come through from London was told by the camp commander that he was to be let out. First thing next morning he would report to the guardroom, where he could collect his belongings and his papers, which would include a travel voucher through to his destination. Then, punctually at seven fifteen, or seven at some camps, the gate would open. The morning air would seem better outside.

There would be a police check at the harbour, and a ticket to Liverpool or Fleetwood to be handed out. Once aboard the steamer, the ex-internee would be a private citizen once more, bound only by the restrictions besetting all aliens in wartime. He could not proceed beyond his port of arrival in the United Kingdom without first reporting to the police; documents would need to be checked and stamped before the next stage of the journey could begin. To most, it was a long way home.

The day for which a man had yearned for so many months would largely be spent waiting around: waiting for a boat to pull out, waiting for an official, queueing for a bite of food bought with the pocket money given him by welfare funds for the journey; waiting for a train, which would almost certainly be late;

queueing for a bus; waiting for a first view of a never-forgotten street. Waiting, just waiting.

At the end of his journey, whether it was home or merely an accommodation address, there was little time before he had to register with the local police. It was indeed all a matter of form. It could hardly be otherwise.

Thousands of men had been collected, thousands released within the year. Not all went back to the life from which they had been taken: some had volunteered for the Army; some had gone to Canada or Australia, and nearly 500 Italians had been lost in the sinking of the *Arandora Star*. A few secured release to emigrate, risking a hazardous sea journey to get to some country where no sirens sounded. But all such groups were small; the substantial majority of the freed men went back to their old surroundings.

One of the most significant statistics that remain is dated 1 March 1941. It is headed 'Return of Kosher Internees' and gives their total in the Manx camps as 395 men at that date. The phrase is possibly ambiguous; the word kosher could be used to mean an internee who opted for kosher food, and there would doubtless be Jews who did not. However, the figure is important in the way it suggests that the number of Jews left in the camps put them decidedly in the minority. This meant that all the original Category C internees had gone, and a high percentage of the Bs had also been released, for the bulk of them had been Jews. They were no longer the largest group behind the wire.

With the releases, much of the character and many of the characters had gone from the camps, for these men had created something of a colourful life for themselves in the suspended animation of internment. The Olympic athlete who had worn the British singlet at the Berlin games and then worn it defiantly in Hutchinson Camp had gone back; he had been a victim of mixed ancestry. The warrant officer, a veteran from the First World War, who had stood every morning with bemedalled chest in his makeshift uniform outside the guardroom at his camp, saluting and claiming his right to release, had also gone. He had brought his medals into internment with him and had proudly worn them on his way out again. There were others like him, men interned in the officers' rig of the British merchant navy, who had spent their working lives under the red ensign; often they were British, they thought British, they spoke only English; their parents had merely forgotten to take out British papers years and years ago when they arrived as refugees at the end of the last century. There had been a number of such cases collected in the crisis days of the previous summer. Such men had now vanished back to normality.

The old and the sick had been released fairly quickly; the men who had been born or lived principally in Britain, speaking only English, were going; the C Class had gone and the B was being re-examined; the men with a war contribution—as owners or factory-workers, scientists or research people—were quickly out. Authority had listed eighteen different categories for release; steadily it could be widened. Until it came to their turn, the men left behind could only hope.

The younger men who played in the inter-camp football league—the games were often played at Onchan, with its field inside the outer wire—had mostly gone, and the enthusiasts who had played their improvised *boule* on the green at Hutchinson had also departed. It is doubtful if they ever replaced the brass bedstead knobs that they had originally used for the balls. Almost everything that was usable in the houses had been used in those early days; linoleum from the floor, chair legs, curtains, even a floorboard—all could be used for painting cut-outs, for wood carving, for a sail to a toy boat and so on. Interned victims of war had behaved like this since the days of the Napoleonic troops languishing in Dartmoor.

One of the first of the colourful eccentrics to be awarded his liberty had been an elderly gentleman at Palace Camp, an elocution expert who was supposed to have given lessons in public speaking to the King, a fact that had not saved him from internment when the stampede started in the great crisis. He was a health food faddist and must have seemed an oddity to some of his pupils in Buckingham Palace, where he was said to have taught singing and elocution for several years. He saw in the dandelion the embodiment of all the gastronomic virtues, and during his spell behind the wire he was allowed out for long daily walks, accompanied by a guard, picking bunches of his favourite leaves. According to the London *Daily Mail*, the lover of dandelions was Signor 'Gaetno' (Gaetano) Loria. He is thought to have appeared under a different name when he came up before one of the early tribunals on the island, when he repeated his claim to a connection with Buckingham Palace. When enquiries were made, it appeared that authority had never heard of him.

He was one of the first of the Walter Mitty brigade with whom internment camps were littered. However, one of the first Italians to be taken in, he was one of the first out.

An internee who aroused much interest was Dr Gerhard Bersu, a German professor of archaeology. A man of international standing, he had done his first notable work back in 1911, excavating Roman pottery kilns in Bavaria. In the 1920s he was director of an important German archaeological centre. In 1935 he was dismissed by Hitler. Three years later he was in Wiltshire, near Salisbury, excavating an Iron Age farmstead. Soon after the beginning of the war, he and his wife were interned as enemy aliens. Then, when the married camp was started in Port St Mary, they were transferred there and lived in internment throughout the war. The Professor's short, chubby figure did not suggest that he could climb lithely in and out of 'digs', but he was a man of high distinction, and word came from London that he need not waste his time while interned. Permissions were sought, funds were provided by learned societies, Chief Inspector Cuthbert gave his blessing, and so from 1941 onwards a series of what were regarded as outstanding excavations were organized and carried out under Bersu's direction by volunteer parties from the camps, watched by armed guards. The bizarre circumstances did not worry the academics; the wife, Maria Bersu, was responsible for the initial survey of the sites, Gerhard Bersu directed the dig. They were a remarkable couple, seemingly immersed in their work and totally happy, unaware, it seemed, that Europe was at war. Never once did they apply for release. The result was the excavation of two Celtic roundhouses and a Viking fort. The timelessness of wartime internment made it possible to give each project an exceptionally long and detailed investigation, and the archaeologist was happy, providing only that he could get his regular supply of snuff.

Professor Bersu died in 1964, and the full details of his work in the Isle of Man were not published until eleven years after that. His was nothing if not a highly specialized internment. His fascination with holes in the ground, his expert knowledge of their contents, and his wife's urge to catalogue and map every inch of them, must have made them an odd pair to the troops who at first guarded them.

To anyone involved with the camps, the Bersus embodied the permanent things of peace. The rumours around the island belonged to the grimmer reality of war. Even as the Bersus started their first preliminary work, it was noticed among Manx officials how the Peveril Camp population out at Peel was steadily decreasing. The inmates were transferring, mainly to Mooragh in Ramsey. Curiosity and speculation were answered by Herbert Morrison, Home Secretary, in the House of Commons. Special legislation, he explained, was necessary before British subjects or non-enemy aliens could be sent out of the United Kingdom; the Isle of Man was not a part of the UK, but it was plain that, in the event of an invasion, some people would be smaller security risks if they were on an island. Up to a thousand people were involved.

All persons of enemy nationality were classed as enemy aliens who could be liable to internment under the Royal Prerogative in a State of War. This covered the rank and file of the internees held in the Isle of Man, in Canada and Australia and in transit camps on the British mainland. Aliens unfriendly to the country's cause, but whose country was not at war with Britain, could be detained under Article 12.5a of the Aliens Order. This was the category that found itself going to Peel and in some cases to prisons in Britain. British subjects considered a potential danger could be detained under Article 18B of the Defence Regulations. A number of these men were members of the British Union of Fascists who would also soon be going to the Isle of Man. So, explained Morrison, the Isle of Man Detention Bill was on its way.

12

Here Come the Fascists

On 22 April 1941 the Manx papers revealed that the internees at Peel had now been transferred to Ramsey and that some 800 British Fascists would arrive shortly. A few weeks later, on 6 May, the *Mona's Herald* stated that the Peveril camp was being prepared for the 18B arrivals. Two roads were to be partially closed to public traffic, and Peel residents who would thus be cut off from the town would be issued with special passes to enable them to use the road. In the event authority was lenient. Not only did the appropriate residents get their passes, but members of the Peel Bowling Club, whose green could be reached only through the camp entrance, were given credentials to add to their membership cards. The perimeter of the camp was strengthened. People in Peel wishing to drive north to Kirk Michael and Ramsey had to detour through Ballaquane Road, as the Peveril Road, which was part of the main coast road, was blocked.

Although the Manx police would not be responsible for guarding the camp, which would be a matter for the military, their numbers were woefully small for the extra duties that Peveril brought with it. At the start of the war the police strength at Peel had consisted of little more than one sergeant, two constables and one police cadet, with reliefs. When the nature of the camp was to change from housing internees to taking the detainees, the need for more men in the police was the more apparent. In law an internee was a person immuned in an interior locality, with no permission to leave the area. A detainee was one to be kept in custody. The difference was fundamental. So in May 1941 the decision was taken to appoint eight auxiliary police constables, at £3 a week each.

On Saturday 10 May the Isle of Man Steam Packet office telephoned through from Fleetwood reporting that 550 Fascists were arriving at noon on the following Monday, escorted by three officers and 143 other ranks. They would leave the port at six in the evening *en route* to the Isle of Man. The steamer would be the *Lady of Mann*.

Monday evening it was, but there was some delay at the start, for the railway porters at the Fleetwood docks refused to handle the luggage, thus holding up the embarkation. It was eleven at night before the ship tied up at the King Edward Pier at Douglas, which had been closed to the public. She had been escorted by a naval boat throughout the journey.

Rumours of the arrival of the Fascists had been around in the town all day, and from mid-evening people gathered in the road to the pier. Many drifted away as the fine evening of late spring darkened into nightfall and there was no sign of activity, but a small crowd remained in the hope of giving the new arrivals a warm and unfriendly reception. As the *Lady of Mann* tied up, a large slogan, crudely chalked, could be read on her upperworks through the gloom: 'MOSLEY FOR PEACE'. An ostensibly friendly speech started to come through a loud-hailer, and one Manx newspaper reported that three cheers for the island were called for from the ship's company. This was too much for the waiting Manxmen, who booed and shouted their derision. There was an attempt at singing from the ship and an effort to start spelling out Mosley's name in a massed chant. It did not work; the catcalls from the shore put it to silence.

The vocal argument died down; the new arrivals spent the night on board. The late prowlers on the front went home. It was six the next morning when the men disembarked. They were then marched in batches along the North Quay to the railway station, each batch under heavy guard.

The town was quiet; little traffic moved before the rush hour; the streets were mainly empty, except for the police, a Steam Packet man or two, the occasional early worker and a newspaper reporter. Some of the marchers were seen to be wearing ribbons from the 1914 war; some wore Union Jacks as armbands; they were later described as a spirited lot, shouting taunts and exchanges with any onlookers who seemed interested. Later that day a local newspaper quoted an eye-witness who saw the arrival at Peel. He had expected to see men of strong convictions, he said, but most of them seemed 'nitwits' with little to commend them. The word was his; he did not explain how he arrived at so quick a judgement.

The operation was completed by mid-morning. A new word was added to the Manx records. No longer did the Internment Camps Division detail only the number of internees; it now added the men of the Peel camp, listed separately, as detainees. At the end of May they totalled 739. They were the wild men at the extremes of politics; some had sinister intent and would be highly dangerous given the chance. They were by no means all the potential terrorists whose cards had been marked in the files of British security. Some were in even tighter and less comfortable security on the mainland, in prison.

One Fascist was conspicuously absent from the main party of internees; he was absent for the whole of the war. Despite the local belief to the contrary, Oswald Mosley was never on the island, other possibly than in peacetime. He spent the critical part of the war in Brixton, the remand prison in south London, where he had ample opportunity to see and hear the air raids on London. He was later transferred to Holloway to join his wife, spending the rest of the war in a flat in an unoccupied wing of the women's prison.

This did not prevent the Manx from quietly speculating that the British blackshirt leader was in Peel. Years later, in 1980, when the writer was researching and writing a book on the history of the Isle of Man Steam Packet, he met a number of the line's retired ship's captains. Two of them were able to assure him that they had personally brought Mosley over to the island during the war. The myth died hard among Manxmen. The fact is: none of Mosley's immediate circle was detailed in the Isle of Man.

13

Disorder at the Palace

In the early days of June 1941 there were about 1,200 men in Palace Camp, Douglas, almost all of them Italians. Eleven months earlier, at the peak of the collection into internment, it had held 2,900.

The men split sharply into two main groups, the Fascists and the anti-Fascists. No amount of careful segregation, putting the groups into different houses, as far apart as possible, could prevent the snarling and bickering that would burst out periodically between the factions. From the start there had always been plenty of vocal political argument in the camps; men, some of whom had fought Franco in the Spanish Civil War, had plenty to say at finding themselves now shut up by the British. In the camps for Germans, the Nazis shouted their victory slogans and sang their songs; peace by conquest was just around the corner. The Communists sneered and talked openly of the break-up of the western world, a tune they were to change by high summer when Russia was attacked. The fire had gone out of the Jew-baiting, partly because few were now left inside. On the surface, most of the internees were perhaps noisy but seemed largely resigned to their position.

At Palace, however, the volatile Italian temperament could always flare up in an outbreak of fighting. It was inevitable that, as time went on and the screening and releasing process went on with it, the tough element, the hardcore types, became an ever larger proportion of the men remaining. Those who could safely be returned to civilian life were steadily released; not so the men who had opted for repatriation, not so the trouble-makers.

Small wonder that a disturbance occurred at Palace Camp on the night of 11 June 1941, the first anniversary of Italy's entry into the war. The Fascists in Palace celebrated noisily, although only they knew what they had to rejoice about. Late that night three hooded men in their early twenties forced their way into a bedroom which contained one of the pro-British Italians and proceeded to attack him violently. The victim was an engineering designer in his fifties who had left the Fascisti twelve years earlier; the idea, it was revealed in evidence later, was 'to make a good Fascist of him'.

The man was badly hurt and put in hospital. On 17 June the Douglas police charged the trio with grievous bodily harm. The men came up in court and received six months' hard labour apiece, served in Douglas Prison.

The camps added yet another burden to the hard-pressed police force. Camps meant visitors, and visitors meant supervision.

From soon after the start of internment in the island the Home Office arranged a permit system whereby relatives could visit an internee, their permit stating the number of visits they could make while it lasted. On arrival the visitor had to give the address at which she would be staying, and her permit would be marked with the time she could remain, staying at the same place. This system endured for the length of the war except for a break at Peel when visits were banned for a time following a riot. Authority allowed emergency permits to be issued if an internee was seriously ill.

All interviews between visitors and internees took place in the presence of an Army Intelligence Officer, of which there was at least one attached to every camp, and sometimes several more. It was very unlikely that they were lone hands. Very unlikely. It was at all times necessary to know what was going on.

There was one thing the men's camps had in common; the standard of their staffing was not to be compared with the Horse Guards Parade. This is not to suggest that the soldiers were indolent or dishonest as a bunch; far from it. They simply were not first-class troops, and a clutch would contain the inevitable bad egg. At the start of internment the officers had largely come from the Retired List, who wanted only to get back into the action but had age against them. The men were not picked from those with the making of front-line soldiers. Later, as the war developed, authority drafted in men who had been badly wounded and were no longer first choice for battle. A Welsh Guards officer, Captain V. G. North, who had been wounded in World War I, was attached to the administration at Onchan, where he was much respected by men and internees; he died on the island, and the Italians worked a design of his regimental badge over his grave in the parish churchyard.

Petty pilfering and similar offences were too common among the guard troops. There was even a long case of a camp commander who was charged by court martial with theft; he was acquitted. Doubtless military discipline and behaviour differed from one camp to another. Nor were the troops solely to blame; in November 1941 a civilian clerk aged sixty from the south of England was sentenced to two months in prison for stealing money belonging to Onchan internees. In retrospect it seems a light sentence.

The Douglas police, busy on so many fronts, kept watch as best they could from the outside. They reported that troop discipline was very slack at Palace and Metropole, where there had been thefts from military stores, and blankets had been stolen. On the night of 2 June 1941, a report maintained, the guard at both camps were asleep in the guardrooms. At various times working parties returning to base were not searched and had been seen carrying parcels. On other occasions guardrooms had been locked.

After Aldershot, Caterham or Catterick, the Isle of Man was indeed a soft touch.

In the middle of war and air raids, the island certainly seemed a land of peace and plenty. The British public read about it enviously as the occasional question came up in Parliament, when the Minister of Food would be asked if he was aware that Germans interned in Douglas had meat on five days a week and cheese on two, and whether he would arrange for British citizens to have priority. The reply that these matters were laid down in the Geneva Convention to which civilized countries adhered was not much consolation to a citizen who could take the whole of his weekly cheese ration at one meal. In the big industrial areas there was a general conviction that the island was luxuriating in the lotus life.

This idea was encouraged by newspapers whose writers recognized that there was a good story in a week-end on the Isle of Man and who persuaded the editor to send them there. The result would be a colourful account of the uncooked hams, the great hunks of beef, the sides of lamb, the pork and bacon, all gaily displayed in the Douglas shops. Some food items, rationed on the mainland, were more readily available on the island, and the writers were quick to point this out.

What they failed to mention was the simple fact that the Manx lived on an island based on farming and surrounded by fish, and that their only other income came almost exclusively from tourism, which had vanished with the war. There was no organization to export the surplus lamb crop; the greenhouses could not sell all their produce; the herds of cattle produced more milk than was needed by a holiday island where there were now no holiday-makers. The economy was out of joint.

The *Sunday Express* produced a list showing the diet officially applied to the internment camps since October 1940. This was mouth-watering to the mainland reader. It showed that every internee was entitled to four ounces of meat on five days a week, ten ounces of fish on two, and a daily intake of twelve ounces of bread, four of flour, fourteen of potatoes and four of fresh vegetables; all this with an ounce of cheese twice a week, in addition to small items that included jam. Parliamentary assurances that it was all right and proper did not stop the grumbling.

The new administration at the Rushen women's camps, appointed in May 1941, was soon making some much-needed alterations. The labour exchange idea, based on mutual co-operation and backed by coins cut from cornflake packets, all so enthusiastically described by Ruth Borchardt, was steadily giving way to a rationalized work scheme run by the camp authorities. A centre was developed at Collinson's Café where women obtained material for their handicraft or handed in finished work; the camp took the goods and sold them either at the shop in Port Erin or at the internees' central shop on the front in Douglas. The money from the sale was credited to the individual internee's account in the camp bank. The raw material given her had been paid by the Camp Welfare Account, and the purchase price depended on how much the authority had to recover and how much the worker was to receive.

Work schemes were soon of top priority. They ranged from weaving and dressmaking to pig-keeping, seaweed collection and fertilizer production. Poultry food was made from kitchen waste, nettles and crushed seashells. Toy-making and shoe-repairing flourished, as did the gymnasium, physical fitness and dancing classes held regularly at Collinson's Café.

Internees, ever eager for a little extra, sold goods direct to local residents, just as in the early days of the exchange scheme. The camp authorities watched this traffic with discretion; where it became blatant, the local purchaser would be prosecuted. But summonses were kept to a minimum as it was important that internees were kept at work.

There was now a little more money in circulation from the camp bank as the rates of pay for work in the kipper and fish factory, and the like, had been fixed at 1s. 8d. (8p.) a day, and this was soon agreed for domestic work in the camp. Some internees also received money by post from outside, and this was put to their credit. So in order to prevent the growth of a two-tier society, the Commandant decreed that a woman could draw out only £1 from her account—if she had it—in any one week. If she wished to shop over this limit, the shopkeeper had to present an invoice, which would be stamped if approved, a development of the system worked out by C. R. Ducker, the Douglas accountant.

Life improved for the seaside landladies as the summer of 1941 developed. The northern factory-workers on the mainland, sometimes sleepless from air raids, needed a break and needed it badly. The daily steamer from Fleetwood started filling up; the Steam Packet suddenly announced an extra sailing at week-ends for the remainder of the summer. There were even cases when a ship had to leave would-be travellers behind for lack of space. Compared with the happy days before the war, it was a mere trickle of custom; compared with the disaster of the 1940 season, it was a welcome windfall.

The visitors were not disappointed. Certainly they found far more in the shops than they would have found back home. To them it seemed that a stroll down Strand Street, Douglas, centre of the town's main shopping area, was as invigorating as a walk along the Promenade.

The sight of so much food produced another headache for the long-suffering Manx police. There was an outbreak of food-smuggling, and this meant more searching, more baggage inspection, more form-filling and more prosecutions. It was strictly forbidden to take food off the island. Anyone caught in the act would be fined and the booty confiscated. Such miscreants were doing the poor a good turn, for the food they surrendered on the Douglas quayside went straight up the hill to an old people's home where it was always gratefully received by the matron. A tolerant policeman would usually let a visitor board the daily steamer with a modest quantity of two foodstuffs. Kippers were plentiful, and a few pairs made a better present back home than any of the three-legged trinkets to be bought in the souvenir shops. Tomatoes, which had almost disappeared on the mainland, were still in excess production, and a pound or two could be spared.

A little, it seemed, was tacitly allowable. But prosecutions for attempted food-smuggling on a larger scale became common-place. A typical example occurred at the end of July, when a Scottish woman was picked up at the pierhead. She was trying to take home ten pounds of jam, seven of sugar, three of margarine, more than a pound of cooking fat and nearly a pound of tea. This was too much of several good things. The result was a fine of £3. The goods took their turn in the waiting cupboards at the home up the hill.

The happy trickle of holiday trade continued into September. Not until then did the Steam Packet suspend its extra sailings.

The Manx welcomed another type of visitor during 1941. The Home Office in London approved a scheme whereby police from blitzed area in the north of England could be moved to the Isle of Man for short spells to carry out light duties at Peveril and

Rushen Camps. This would help to take a little of the strain off the Manx force and would at the same time give the visiting police a short break.

A sergeant and ten constables arrived in August, for a fortnight's duty. They were from the Lancashire police and were the first arrivals. Their wives came with them, and lodgings were provided in Peel and Port St Mary.

The scheme continued into the following spring, a busman's holiday for policemen. It was a great success with the men lucky enough to be drafted to it; it gave the man a change from the raids and it gave the wife a holiday.

From the start the original idea produced some rather heavy banter; one very senior officer wrote: 'The only criticism I can offer is that the scheme might be in charge of a chief constable as I could do with a month in the Isle of Man.' Another chief ended his letter of approval with the jovial, 'I suppose they don't require any chief constables on the island?'

Very soon the tone of the correspondence had changed; a wordy war on costs and who paid for them had broken out.

14

Camp Newspapers

Nothing revealed the feelings of the internees and the life they shared together more clearly than the newspapers produced in the Manx camps. The first, the most widely circulated and the longest lasting was the *Onchan Pioneer*.

There were others. Legend indeed maintains that most units had their own papers. This is possible, but highly unlikely, and we know only of two other papers apart from Onchan's. No trace has been found of the *Mooragh Times* which was said to have been printed entirely in German and which, if it existed at all, must have related to the early days of internment; nor has a camp newspaper been traced in Peel, which did, however, have a curious publication, the *Peveril Guardsman*, intended not for the detainees but for the troops who guarded them. Port Erin was said to have had its own paper, the *Awful Times*. No copy was ever traced, and from the first it seemed very improbable that women whose common language was German would have chosen a sardonic English pun for a title. The belief persisted, but the files show that the *Awful Times* was a joke perpetrated by an ex-internee in a letter to the *Onchan Pioneer* some time after her release from the island.

However, in addition to the *Onchan Pioneer* two other camp papers have survived, the *Sefton Review* and *The Camp*, which was published in Hutchinson; they were probably the only three ever produced.

The first issue of the *Onchan Pioneer* was dated 27 July 1940, when the camp was getting on for two months old. It was almost entirely in German and consisted of six duplicated pages on poor foolscap. The front page started with a welcoming message to the paper and its readers from the Commander, Major C. R. C. Marsh, for whom the internees seem to have developed a considerable respect. A fortnight later the paper announced—in English—that the Major had been promoted and was leaving the camp. The editorial went on to report how he had 'worked hard to alleviate hardship and improve the conditions of our internment'. It ended in boyish fashion—'Three cheers for Major Marsh'.

This cheerful fourth-form attitude to life is reflected in issue after issue of the *Pioneer*, and it set the mood for the few copies remaining of the other camp publications. The Head, the prefects seemed to be saying, is a jolly decent chap. The sceptic could wonder how much of this heartiness was for external consumption, for the *Pioneer* had enterprise and seems to have built up a small mailing list outside the wire that surrounded it. But the desperate desire to be up and working in the war effort comes through in page after page, issue after issue, second only to the yearning for freedom and vitally linked up with it. Sometimes naïvely expressed through the words of a man who thinks in one language and writes in another, it gives a sad feeling of frustration and emptiness. 'What is our station, Mr Churchill?' asked a headline writer. 'It can't be the idleness of an internment camp.'

In its next issue the paper asks once more: 'Has this country in its terrible struggle no use for the strength of our hearts, the ability of our brains, the might of our work?' The plea went on, month after month, sometimes in English, sometimes in German, the sad rhetoric in which it was phrased detracting nothing from it. Adopting the old formula of the Open Letter, the *Pioneer* assured the Under Secretary of State for the Home Office that it had noticed with pleasure how he had acknowledged the friendly attitude of the internees in a statement he had made in the House of Commons. 'We are and remain friends of Britain,' it assured him, 'deeply and sincerely attached to her and her people.'

By the end of September, when the Battle of Britain was slashing white lines across the skies of Kent, the editor assured readers, 'Britain's cause is our cause.' A month later the paper was advocating an Aliens' Labour Corps, a mobile work unit that could build shelters, take on special construction jobs and do similar non-combative work. It would not add to any unemployment problem, and it spoke of the 'natural reluctance of British war workers to change their place of residence'.

The *Pioneer* took on a very serious tone in its November issues, for it had much to write about. It moved from making pleas to parading facts, publishing a statistical survey of its own internees. It analysed 803 camp members, ignoring all Onchan internees who had no calling, all students, all those who had enlisted for non-combatant Army work and all who were waiting for emigration to the United States. This exercise showed that the camp consisted of 93 graduate engineers, 347 skilled workers and craftsmen, 270 merchants, and 93 professionals, including physicians, lawyers, artists, writers, clergy and teachers. No mention of musicians, of which Onchan had many.

The categories were broken down. A surprising statement claimed that twelve of Onchan's men had been in domestic service. No doubt these classifications could be challenged; there seems not to have been a labourer, all workers in the building industry being skilled; fifteen clerical workers were listed, presumably ranking as skilled. As Joad, who was in fashion at the time, would have said: it all depends on what you mean by skilled. However, while there could be quibbles over the categories, the main message was plain: a great deal of potential talent was being wasted. The unnamed writer finished with an urgent plea: interned men could not find employment for themselves; an organization should be set up by the British authorities to include and direct internee abilities into the war effort. 'Why not enlist our knowledge and abilities?' he implored.

Early in December the *Pioneer* summarized the community work that had been done since June. The campaign to relieve monotony started with the opening of a shoemaker's shop early in July, among many other activities. Two thousand boot repairs had been completed by the middle of November, half of them free. By the end of the year this work would be running at a rate of eighty pairs a day. The Onchan Camp's Welfare Fund had already received £35 contributed from shoeshop receipts. Walter Mueller, who ran the shop, was already making warm winter slippers from waste.

Other shops had quickly followed. A tailor started up, doing repairs. Then came the dry cleaner's and the barber's shop. This last was not unexpectedly a huge success. In their first four weeks the barbers carried out 423 haircuts. Among those pioneering developments was a joiner's shop; without it there would have been difficulty fitting out the houses where the other craftsmen were installed. Additionally, the joiners were able to build poultry-houses and rabbit-hutches, to make blackboards and stretchers and tables. The work had been started by two experienced joiners who had since taken on two young beginners. At the same time an allotment section was being built up; the gardens were well tended; the rearing of chickens, ducks and turkeys was being started. Allotments were being marked out, cut, dug and prepared for the next season.

'It is only to be hoped that those who sow shall not harvest,' wrote the *Pioneer* in its familiar tone of hopeful melancholy. Meanwhile there were encouraging signs. Men at various levels in the camp were already being released, sometimes causing sudden elections to camp offices as they fell vacant.

The paper did not deal solely with internment and its frustrations. It covered the news from the outside world, interpreting it always as it involved the plight of its own readers. It had been pleased when the Home Office was given the responsibility for managing the camps; it quoted official figures of releases and revealed that the *Guardian* had reported that Nazis and anti-Nazis had been put together in internment camps in Australia. The same thing, it said, could be applied to conditions at Huyton. The *Jewish Chronicle* was quoted as saying that 14,250 Jewish internees had been released and 7,000 were still held; this on 25 April 1941. The *Pioneer's* editors appeared to be free in their inspection of the more serious, opinion-forming papers, and they made liberal use of them.

The *Pioneer* then gave details of Onchan's Popular University, not perhaps as ambitious as that at Hutchinson but impressive considering the conditions. It announced an 'internee artists' exhibition' to which entry would be by programme, priced 1d. It reported the first meeting with wives at Derby Castle Hotel, gave the result of camp sports meetings and reported a grand concert at Derby Castle, organized by musicians from the camp, with proceeds to welfare funds, and with the National Anthem to finish the evening.

When it wished, the *Pioneer* would turn to welfare matters. It campaigned for improved arrangements for daily walks for those internees who did not go in for organized games; Onchan's recreational area, although pleasant enough, was wet and unsuitable for walking parties on rain-soaked days; walks should be organized outside the camp. Professor Otto Kestner, one of the few academics in Onchan, was a dietician of repute. He laid down that there was a protein deficiency and a lack of Vitamin A in the food. With scientific detachment he urged readers to concentrate on fish; if meat seemed inadequate, they should take 'lots' more bread, although, he added, 'the bread itself is not palatable to the German taste'. But there was nothing heated about his contribution; he was not arguing that internees were being underfed; he was querying the intake of the right nourishment.

In other issues the paper appealed for books, especially scientific books, for the camp library; later it reported gleefully that the Society of Friends had donated a book-binding kit. This was installed in House 45 and was soon being used to renovate library stock.

Regularly the little journal printed letters it received from outside. Prominent people wrote and thanked the editor for the latest copy of the paper and wished it and its readers well. The occasional pound note would be attached to the letter. The *Pioneer* always needed money, being produced as it was in a community where a penny was important, and it was not above asking for a small sub from any sympathizer.

It made much of the achievements of its Popular University when that remarkable institute had completed six months of active life. Professor Otto Liebreich of the London School of Economics contributed an appreciation of the work done. It revealed that there were 30 different courses and that 600 students attended daily. In the first half year 4,500 classes had been held, and on average every internee had attended more than 60. Even preparations for Christmas 1940 did not stop the steady flow of learning. But Christmas was an opportunity for the internees to make seasonal contact with the outside world, even if only by post, and to make things that might earn a mite of cash. The camp authorities encouraged the design and production of Christmas cards; these were stencilled, hand coloured and even sold to the Manx public.

For its Christmas issue the *Onchan Pioneer* started with a

seasonal letter from the Reverend John Duffield, the Vicar of Onchan, regarded by internees as the camp's padre. Onchan was later to change to Italian inmates, whose priests settled in the Park Hotel, which became known locally as the Vatican. Where release was offered, many rabbis and priests among the internees refused it, preferring to remain and help the other inmates. From the start they had held Duffield in very high regard. In an editorial the camp journal wrote of him as a 'real Christian' and said that the Jews and Catholics among them could feel the warmth of his simple faith. His Christmas letter began with the words 'Dear Friends' and was followed by one in German contributed by an interned rabbi.

The *Onchan Pioneer* continued until 20 July 1941, when Issue 47 was its last. It had started almost exactly a year earlier, with six pages; it finished with fourteen, including four as a supplement, *Onchan Camp Youth*, a junior section originally given over to inter-camp sport.

The paper finished because Onchan was closing down for a time and the internees were being transferred to other camps. The last issue was remarkable for its tone; the men had become proud of their handiwork, and they actually resented the closing. 'The spirit of this camp was probably the best at all possible in an internment camp,' lamented the last editorial, which went on to say that there had been goodwill on both sides; it once again bestowed much praise on John Duffield. It ended by bemoaning the fact that the victims of Fascism would be turning over the fruits of what they had sown with their own work and money to what would be an Italian Fascist camp. They assumed they would be making way for Italians; the very thought seemed humiliating.

The *Pioneer* left one lasting memorial behind it: the quality of its drawings. Even after more than forty years it is impossible to look at them without realizing the deep feeling of loneliness behind almost every one of them. They are work of very high quality, from the stencil of a duplicating machine. A succession of artists contributed to the paper; some worked for it for many months. Bertram, whose work was choicely simple, making his point with the minimum of fuss, was sketching away in the *Pioneer*'s final number, meaning that no release was yet in sight for him. Others were luckier.

In its very last issue the paper carried a short report from London, dealing with the 1941 summer exhibition at the Royal

Academy. It claimed proudly that ten ex-internees from Onchan were among the artists on show.

Certainly a number of Onchan men were no strangers to the Academy. None of them had the standing of Kurt Schwitters, who had been in Hutchinson, whose collages gave him an international reputation, and perhaps none of them attracted the respect shown to Fred Uhlman, but many of these refugee Germans whose work appeared in the *Pioneer* had solid standing as professional artists. Kaufman had exhibited at the Academy; Markiewicz was previously a portrait painter who had exhibited in London; Nonnenmacher made his name mainly as a sculptor, as did Elkan, whose work is in several European and American galleries. Bertram exhibited at a number of Continental galleries, his drawings fetching good prices.

The Germans who were the first internees at Onchan included not only a number of artists but several musicians, some of whom subsequently made considerable reputations for themselves. Curiously, not a single musician is listed in the statistical survey that the Onchan internees conducted among themselves; yet ephemeral papers that have survived from the camp include the programme of a 'grand concert', held at the Derby Castle on 8 October 1940, starting at the significantly early hour of 5.30. Among the performers named is Hans Schidlof, who later became one of the leading instrumentalists of the day and is a founder member of the Amadeus Quartet. (His full name is Hans Peter Schidlof but he dropped the Hans early in his career.)

Schidlof is in many ways typical of some thousands of internees. Born in Austria in 1922 of Jewish parents, he was sent to Britain in December 1938 to escape the clutches of Hitler's rampant anti-Semitism. He was rounded up and interned in London when only seventeen. After a spell at Prees Heath, where he met Norbert Brainin, the Viennese who later became his colleague in the Quartet, he was sent on to Onchan, where he met Siegmund Nissel and many musicians, some already well established and others to make names in the future.

Nissel was the third Viennese in what became the Amadeus Quartet. They met the fourth member, Martin Lovett, when they were later studying under Max Rostal. The man who played the key part in merging the talents of the four musicians was Ferdinand Rauter, the pianist, whom Schidlof had first met in a London police station when both men were taken in during the original round-up. Rauter and Schidlof spent part of their time at Onchan working on sonatas. Years later Schidlof said that while in the camp he took lessons in musical theory and harmony and went to many of the lectures on music, which were of a very high standard. The camp gave the young students the rare opportunity of learning from older men who were already specialized musicians.

Schidlof's release, in 1941, resulted largely from the testimonials provided by Sir Adrian Boult and Myra Hess. He said much later that he considered Onchan's studies had 'finished' his education as well as giving him his first taste of playing to an audience.

Hutchinson Camp produced a straightforward newspaper called, simply enough, *The Camp*. It made its first appearance on 21 September 1940 and was issued somewhat irregularly, sometimes but once a month. Yet it put '2nd Year' on its masthead for its issue of 28 July 1941, when the paper was certainly not a year old.

Surviving copies of *The Camp* are rarities; such specimens as the writer has seen suggest that it had little or no space for illustrators so that it lacked the immediate visual appeal of the *Onchan Pioneer*. This might be thought curious, for Hutchinson had a number of professional artists among its internees. Kurt Schwitters, the Dadaist who was both poet and artist and who invented the wild art form Merz, adopted England after he was released from internment there and eventually died at Ambleside, where his work can still be seen. While interned in Hutchinson, he painted a most impressive portrait of Fred Uhlman, another internee, who made an international name for himself and became a Royal Academician. It is the only piece of work that has been traced from the Hutchinson camp, apart from some publications of Uhlman's, yet an exhibition of internee art work had been held there within a month of its opening.

Copies of issues for the end of 1941 still survive. They contain some sophisticated drawings, stencilled in two colours, by Baumgaertel, Dzubas, Harold Mahrenholz and L. Meidner among others. A full-page sketch, very neat and professional, shows that for Christmas anyway the Hutchinson camp would even sanction a genteel pin-up. Two issues earlier, in November

1941, the editor, Hans Schulze, sent good wishes to John Duffield, the Onchan vicar who was leaving the island to rejoin the Army as a chaplain. Hutchinson inmates remembered him with affection from his work at Onchan Camp, where many of them were first interned on their arrival in the island. Precisely when the paper faded out is not known for certain. The camp itself went through many changes and contained men of several nationalities before it finally closed in the spring of 1944.

Sefton Camp was the shortest lived of them all, and its newspaper, the *Sefton Review*, was published only from November 1940 to 3 February 1941, during which time it produced seven issues. The men of Sefton were a very different lot from those of Onchan and Hutchinson: they included an unusual percentage of invalids, 42 out of 307 at one time. But the *Sefton Review* was a bright little newspaper. It had ideas. It published details of its editorial birthpangs; it wrote to the Mayor of Coventry offering a gift of toys to families stricken by the notorious air raid, and it received a kindly reply. In the manner of the *Onchan Pioneer*, it wrote to leading politicians. It laughed quite often, and frequently at itself. It apparently had no idea that its February issue would be its last. The end of the camp was unexpected, at least to its inmates.

So camps changed their occupants, and thus changed their personality. Peel was no longer an internment camp; it was specially adapted for detainees. Onchan had started with a population of Germans; it had been orderly and properly behaved, its newspaper reflecting its men. Then it was given over to Italians and became noisier and more high-spirited one day, dejected the next. Its character was to change frequently while it served its purpose for most of the war.

There was great excitement in Onchan at the time of Tobruk; a break-out nearly succeeded but was intercepted at the final cutting of the wires. The incident never ranked as an escape; it was all over too quickly. It was known, too, that there was trouble early in 1943, when some Italians made a strenuous effort to get away. One guard, now resident on the island, recalls the incident as a near-riot. Whatever it was, it called for no outside involvement, and no record of it can be traced.

The last provocative incident at Onchan remembered by men who mounted guard there was a fire in the internees' canteen on a summer night in 1943. Sabotage was suspected but no charge resulted. But, as with the other camps, the Onchan guard remained vigilant, patrolling the wire, usually in pairs. Sentry duties were varied from time to time, in order to inconvenience any internee who was timing the operation with a view to taking advantage of it.

One military duty was occasionally to take internees across to the mainland and guard them down to London, where they were wanted for interrogation. The job was eagerly sought by soldiers who were themselves Londoners or had links with the capital. The routine was to cross over to the mainland on the Monday and arrive in London not later than the next day; this gave the guard the Wednesday off at home or in the town, reporting to Oratory School, which was the collection point, on the Thursday evening. He would then take a party of internees up to Fleetwood on the night train. The general complement of guards was a lance-corporal and three privates to eight internees. In some cases, on arrival down at Euston, they would be met by Metropolitan police, who would then take over. It was all organized, and the soldier had rather more than a day off.

Guards, in the opinion of most internees, were merely civilians doing a dreary job. Relations between them were correct, sometimes cordial; except at the start, there was little or no bullying. One ex-guard vividly recalls an incident in Onchan, when a pair of internees had been sent outside, grass-cutting. They were under guard by a young soldier who suddenly collapsed with what turned out to be appendicitis. The internees returned to camp carrying the soldier between them. His rifle was slung over the shoulder of the internee in the rear.

Providing he obeyed the rules, the life of a long-term internee, like that of a merchant seaman, was nothing if not uneventful. Its greatest curse was that it could become horribly boring; sport, card games and indoor pursuits were all very well, but week after week, month after month, they merely varied a basic monotony.

As far as possible, Giovanni Moneta was reasonably content. He went to English classes and steadily learned the language. He enjoyed his occasional days out on the farm. He was lucky in his living-quarters. The Metropole camp contained two hotels—the Metropole itself and the Alexander, since named the Continental—that were larger than most of those commandeered for the internment camps, so if a man shared a room in either, he had more space around him than if was one of the crowd in a small boarding-house. Moneta was in Metropole itself, sharing with his shipmate Lanzardo Mattio.

Mattio was a deckhand on the SS *Marzocco*, and the pair of them had been together ever since. Like Giovanni, he came from the Isle of Elba, where his family were the bakers serving the village of Marciana Marina.

Because they were in a large hotel, the *Marzocco* crew usually ate together in the sizeable dining-room, rather than in small rooms on their own, but they usually made their own food, having drawn their own rations. In this way they continued with an identity of their own: A-class internees, a ship's crew under their own captain, who presided at table. There was one thing they had completely forgotten about after the outbreak of war: the way they had scuttled their ship and the way they had ended up together in the Metropole. They had forgotten Rotterdam.

It had been the ship's last port of call on its way to Newcastle, where it loaded coal. The town was a shambles from the devastation of the air raids. But it was the place where the crew picked up their mail from home. It would be waiting, *poste restante*. This time there had been no mail. It had simply not arrived in time for their departure. In the events that followed it was forgotten. Then, one day near the end of 1942, it turned up at the Metropole, having been 2½ years in transit.

Its contents were long since out of date. Its arrival caused the only real ripple of excitement in months.

15

A Riot at Peel

The Manx in the small town of Peel had no love for the Peveril Camp in their midst. They called it the Fascist Camp. This it was to a large extent, and it held some highly undesirable characters, but it was not just the presence of Mosleyites that irritated the people of what the Manx call the Sunset City. It was the behaviour of the visiting womenfolk. The islanders were accustomed to the women who secured permits to visit the various camps, and inasmuch as any visitor was welcome, they welcomed them in turn. But the women for the Peel camp were different. They were dubbed arrogant, and many had too much money to spend. They were brash in the way they went round buying up unrationed food and taking it off to the camp. The shopkeepers were unable to tell whether a stranger was a rare holiday visitor or a detainee's woman. The people of Peel watched the descent on their shops and disliked it thoroughly.

The man who most strongly disliked these visitors was A. E. Ostick, who was, among other things, the owner of the Creg Malin Hotel, down on the Promenade, on the opposite side of the Walpole Road from one of the entrances to the camp. It was a tall, severe-looking building and far from beautiful. The island's pubs were not objects of architectural admiration, and the Creg Malin was one of the least attractive of them, possibly because of its size. It was built for slaking thirsts, not for elegance. The womenfolk of the detainees used it as their last port of call before it was their turn to go to the huts to meet their men. They would arrive at the pub with their parcels of food and wait their turn. Sometimes a woman left her children in the care of the hotel staff while she went along for the meeting, held in the presence of an intelligence officer. Then, suddenly, Ostick put his foot down: none of these women was to be served in his hotel. Enough was enough.

Complaints about the camp's visiting womenfolk had been mounting throughout the summer of 1941. The Peel Town Commissioners were assured at their July meeting that the women were pests, creating shortages of supplies in the town. It was alleged that food, not by the pound but by the hundred-weight, was getting into the camp. At the same meeting a member complained that, when the detainees were bathing from the shore, local people were directed away from the beach by the military. He considered it grossly unfair.

Such remarks bred rumour. Much conversational play was made of a court case reported in the local newspapers after a Fascist detainee had sneaked away from a farm working party of which he was a member and was found sitting in the corner of a field with his girl friend and sister-in-law. The two women, both British, were charged with acting in a manner likely to prejudice the discipline of internees. It turned out that one woman was in Peel for a visit to her husband and the other to her man friend. The wife had more than £80 on her when arrested, a large amount of cash in the circumstances in those days. Both were fined. It made bad publicity for the Fascist wives.

Then came another 130 detainees, collected from prisons in different parts of Britain. They were mostly foreigners and not British Fascists. There were no incidents when they docked at Douglas and none when they reached Peel. But it was noticed that they brought with them what one newspaper described as an 'incredible' amount of baggage. By the time this story had been well and truly circulated, it was a luggage mountain indeed.

Importantly, these men were dangerous, and the senior authorities knew it. The problem was to make them really secure, and to secure the town with them. Much confidential material flowed to high places in London, with recommendations. The Peel camp was a time-bomb, and the risk not inconsiderable. It was sensed that there was mischief brewing. And what was the protection? Guards who were not the best of trained troops and a small island police force stretched to the very limit of its capacity—these things were not reassuring. Feelings improved somewhat with the arrival of Major Dunne, the third commander in a camp that had been in existence for scarcely four months as a centre of detainees and that contained some desperate characters. He came with a reputation for standing no nonsense and with a good record behind him. As it turned out, he had arrived too late.

It was in mid-September when the real trouble started, on the night of Wednesday, 17 September 1941. According to a newspaper report a party of about 200 detainees were at a concert in a small hall a few hundred yards out from the camp. All was normal as the men were marched back to the wire, but in the short march three men had managed to slip away from the party in the dusk. The public reaction was immediate. Such a thing could have happened only because of gross casualness; it raised serious question marks about the whole guard system at Peveril. Report said that the men's absence was not noticed until nine o'clock the following morning, suggesting that no sort of count had been made when the party returned to camp. That, however, was the orthodox newspaper version of the escape. It is reasonably certain that the Manx police did not believe it.

There was an elaborate plan for handling escapes, and it moved into action as soon as it was established that a man was missing. Internment Camp Headquarters in Douglas was informed at once and the police were warned; the police procedure was to alert all stations on the island, to tell London, to advise the island's civilian authorities and to contact the naval and military bases and the RAF stations on the Isle of Man. Harbour masters and coastguards were all alerted, and printed descriptions and relevant details of the missing man or men circulated, including clothing—in this case all three men were in brown sports jackets and grey trousers.

A search was launched immediately, and it was soon realized that the men had headed south and gone down to the beach at Glen Maye, a beauty spot about two miles below Peel on the west coast. If they were looking for a boat which they could steal, this was the wrong place. They were later reported at a farm at Ballamoda. There was then a report that a twelve-foot motor fishing-boat, *Sunbeam*, which belonged to a local man, was missing from its moorings in Castletown Harbour, and almost immediately came a message that a small warehouse in School Lane, Castletown, had been broken into and some equipment stolen.

The *Sunbeam* was a modest little boat, being subsequently valued at a mere £40, which even in those days was a poor price for a good fishing-boat. But its owner had obeyed the book. Under the wartime regulations it was compulsory for all boats to be immobilized when left moored. Oars and rowlocks had to be stored away from the craft; if power-driven, the engine had to be put out of action. The owner had done the right thing. There were no sparking plugs.

The trio had put to sea with two pairs of stolen oars. Naval patrol vessels, Manx motorboats and an aircraft took part in a sea search, and a special watch was kept on harbours and anchorages around the island's coast in case the men were forced back. The Irish Sea was no place for a powerless fishing-boat in the last week of September, with the autumnal gales around.

On Saturday afternoon, more than two days after the escape, the men were retaken from their open boat, seven miles off the Calf of Man. They were trying to reach the Irish coast, of whose Mountains of Mourne they would occasionally have had a tantalizing glimpse. They did not know that there had been twenty-four Irish fishing-boats in port at Peel that week: the trio might have had a safer and more comfortable journey that way, for two of them were Irish. They were exhausted and hungry when taken aboard the RN patrol vessel that had first sighted them. They had eaten a bag of apples and nothing else. When searched they were found to be unarmed, with only a trifling sum of money in cash between them. This was sufficiently unexpected to find its way into the records, for detainees were not allowed to have money in camp, although they often obtained it, frequently from local farmers.

The men were given food and drink, landed back at Douglas and were met by a sergeant and a constable of the Manx CID. They were then taken back to the Peveril Camp, arriving at about seven in the evening, guarded by an escort of soldiers and police. All this complied with regulations. If a man gets out; take him back; then charge him later with a common law offence, and take and hold him until the matter is disposed of. But in this case the consequences of the decision to take the men home to Peveril gave the island its most eventful wartime incident to that date.

They were delivered to the camp cells.

On that same week-end Osbert Peake, Member of Parliament and Parliamentary Under Secretary to the Home Office, who had flown over to the Isle of Man, made a tour of inspection of the camps. Peake was a quiet, unobtrusive man, correct in his manner, not unaware of the plight of an internee. In Parliament he had always shown moderation. He represented what might be regarded as the more liberal Home Office attitude to the problem of internment rather than that of the hardliners.

His visit had been arranged earlier; Peveril was merely one of his ports of call. He spent much time in the southern camps; he went on to Peveril on the Saturday afternoon. It was his intention to receive a deputation from the detainees. At least one of the senior authorities in the island had warned against going into the camp. It is thought that Major Dunne, when the Minister arrived, also advised against any such move. But Peake had made up his mind. He was not afraid and the Major went with him. They were greeted with screams of abuse from the British Fascists. They were jostled and had to retreat hurriedly. The noise became such that onlookers gathered in the street, and one said later that the men had appeared to go frantic and 'behaved like maniacs'. A banner appeared, inscribed 'Mosley Give Us Justice'. One report, possibly true, said that the foreigners among the detainees looked on but kept aloof.

Peake was representing disciplined authority, and the Fascists hated him for it. There were hysterical shouts of 'He's a Jew' and 'We want justice'. Obscenities were yelled at him. The Camp Commander was virtually ignored. The Home Office man was the target, and some 200 detainees were said to have been involved.

The mood was sullen and dangerous when the three escapees were brought back to camp from their attempt to get across to Ireland.

Exactly how the riot started is uncertain. The three men who got away were probably heroes to those left behind. After more than two days at liberty, their admirers possibly felt confident that the escape had been successful, and the sight of them returning under guard was a disappointment. The men themselves said later that they were ravenous after their time on the run and that they were refused food on return. This was denied. They could have food, but no hot meal was available.

Soon after their return a substantial number of detainees started a mounting riot. Demonstrators pulled down a stone hedge at the back of the camp, inside the wire. It had been made by building up two lines of any stone or rock available, filling the space between them with earth, thus binding the whole together in a wall high enough to hold sheep or cattle—a typical Manx sod hedge. It was also a useful ammunition dump, quickly torn apart; the pelting of the guard resulted.

By ten at night the riot was in full fury. Every available soldier was called to reinforce the guard on duty. Stones, bottles, plates, lavatory seats, timbers, dustbin lids—anything a man could lay his hands on; the missiles flew over the wire, across Walpole Road, and crashed into the side of the Creg Malin, which because of its sombre size was an easy target. Thirty windows were smashed, and the roadway was littered with rocks and debris. It was a noisy fracas and a strange sight. As darkness fell, the lights surrounding the camp were switched on, lighting up the whole area; a week or two later the local Peel newspaper, whose editor had almost forgotten what illuminations looked like, wrote that the lights had been particularly attractive from the sea. He hoped the town commissioners had taken note and would remember after the war.

The lights and the noise brought out the onlookers. Hundreds of townspeople flocked down to the Promenade to see what was happening. They were held back by a barrier that had been placed hurriedly across the road, so that they could not get too near. What little they could see they heartily disliked. There developed a protest against protests, and loud were the calls for action. Some women in the crowd were evacuees from a bombed town in the north of England, and their opinion of Fascists was loud and lucid.

It was approaching midnight by the time things simmered down. By then some food was said to have been taken from the hotel to the recaptured men, who were in the cells. Meanwhile Lieutenant-Colonel Baggaley, who was Commandant of all the Manx men's camps, had arrived from the Internment Camps HQ, which was in Douglas at Mereside, a private hotel that had been taken over on Empire Terrace.

Peake was reported as being in the Creg Malin and was said to have received a deputation from the Fascists and listened to their complaints for an hour. It was later alleged that when the men crossed the road back to camp they gave the Fascist salute.

The Under Secretary was certainly nothing if not courteous. What would probably have been the majority point of view was pungently put by A. J. Cummings, whose widely read political column in the *News Chronicle* was noted for its normally tolerant and liberal views. He described the riot as a 'scandalous affair' and demanded to know why Peake had tried to appease the rioters as if they were no worse than an excited group of school-boys out for a lark. 'One can imagine what would have happened if the same kind of mutiny had broken out in a prisoner's camp in Germany,' he added. Poor Peake; when it came to internment, it seemed he could do no right.

The tumult and the shouting died; the area outside the camp, down at the start of the Promenade, looked a shambles, with windows smashed and slates broken on the opposite side of the road. The Creg Malin had been an Aunt Sally on which frustrated Fascists could vent their feelings. Ostick, the genial local businessman who ran much of the town's entertainment and was one of the pioneers of motor coach tours on the island, never forgave them. It was the wives who suffered.

Away at the Home Office in London it was stated that a court of inquiry was started immediately.

By Monday morning the debris had already been cleared away by detainees working under guard. Farm work-parties started out from the camp again. By the Wednesday those Fascists who so wished were bathing from the shore, and two brewery lorries were seen delivering the liquid intake to the camp. Coaches left in the afternoon taking detainees to see their wives in Port Erin. It seemed to be business as usual. But soldiers had been stoned in the riot, and the regulations denied them the right to hit back while the trouble was still confined inside the wire. The Manx were angry, very angry.

And unknown to the Manx, and the camp authorities, there was more trouble in store.

16

An Uneasy Week

One very significant event occurred in Peel on Monday 22 September. It went unnoticed while both camp and community slept. At two o'clock in the morning two Manx policemen went to the camp cells and arrested the three men who had escaped. Two were Irish, members of the IRA, which had been active in London during the weeks before the outbreak of war. The third was a member of the British Fascist party.

They were taken to the Isle of Man Prison in Victoria Road, Douglas, and appeared in court before the High Bailiff in the afternoon charged with stealing the motor fishing-boat *Sunbeam*. It was at this appearance that one of the men alleged that they had been refused food and blankets on being brought back to camp that Saturday. They were remanded to the Douglas prison. They were now in the custody of the law. Peveril had finished with them.

On the Thursday two things happened in the developing action at Peel. In London the Home Office issued a statement, broadcast that night by the BBC, saying the inquiry was nearing its completion and that, as soon as its findings were received, appropriate action would be taken. Administrative decisions were being considered that would prevent further disturbances. That affray on Saturday was always a 'disturbance' to the authorities, never a riot. 'It is already clear that some accounts of the disturbances have been exaggerated,' said the statement.

'There was much shouting and disorderly conduct but no assault was directed against any individual. Only two persons were slightly hurt. . . .' The Home Secretary was taking steps to make it clear to detainees that such misbehaviour would not be tolerated.

The Manx listened to the announcement but they were not happy. They had a dangerous mechanism ticking away in their midst, and they did not like it. However, the people of Peel were soon told in the Press that fire hose had been installed in Peveril so that the guards could cool off any future rioters. This was the type of news they wanted to read, but they felt the installation had been made one riot too late. On that same Thursday too, they learned that the guard at the camp had been changed; replacements had been brought in.

Unfortunately the first of these reassuring statements was untrue. It would be interesting to know how it originated, for it appeared with every appearance of authority in one of the island's most respected newspapers. But the installation of fire hose in the Peveril camp was imaginary. There was no way in which the guard could use fire hydrants to quell the ardour of a rioter. The water-supply situation at the camp was in fact a source of some concern to officialdom. The Peel Water Company supplied the town from a small reservoir behind Patrick, about three miles away. The pressure was regulated at the reservoir and was only just adequate for the town's normal use. There were frequent complaints that water was merely trickling from taps on the first floor of houses at the highest end of the town, and later in the war a fire at one of the houses on the top road was put out only after a special journey to Patrick to boost the pressure and thus get an adequate supply. Experienced water engineers who worked in the Peel area have assured the writer that no extra water points or hoses were installed in the camp following the riot. However, the statement no doubt reassured the good citizenry of Peel.

On the Saturday the *Isle of Man Weekly Times* spoke for the island. It was strongly critical of the events of the previous weekend. 'The camp guard,' it said, 'was reinforced, but the officers and men had to face this terrible state of affairs without the power to retaliate. Several soldiers were hit by stones. . . . Officials in this camp have been criticised. We heard it on all sides on Saturday night when civilians called out "Why don't the soldiers fire on these rats?" The Home Office regulations, we believe, do not permit force to be used against these Fascists. . . . We firmly believe that had Captain Arthur Curle, in charge of the guard, been given a free hand the riot would soon have been ended. . . . The public in Peel hate these Fascists. . . ."

Later that same Saturday a senior Scotland Yard officer, Chief Inspector S. M. Ogden, a man with wide and specialized experience of Fascist activities, arrived on the island by air, armed with a brief from the Home Office.

Sam Ogden had joined the Metropolitan Police in 1919, having served throughout the First World War, when he had been commissioned and seen service in Palestine, Gallipoli and France. In the London police he rose to be Chief Inspector at West End Central for three years, having previously been at Vine Street. He knew exactly the type of man he could expect to meet at Peel, having been in charge of collecting a number of them at the outbreak of war.

He had a crowded week-end. He went to the Peveril Camp and had interviews with the military authorities, both on the spot and in Douglas. He spent some time with B. A. Sargeaunt, the Manx Government Secretary, and had talks with Major Young, the Chief Constable. He also talked at length with Chief Inspector Cuthbert, his Scotland Yard colleague now running the Rushen Camp, who, like him, had specialized knowledge of aliens and internment generally.

During the week-end of his visit, rumours of more trouble in the camp circulated widely and were even reported on the BBC. They were subsequently and very emphatically denied, and there is no doubt that, while tempers may have been frayed and while the atmosphere was sullen and resentful, there was no second outbreak of violence. Had there been, Inspector Ogden would have seen it for himself.

There was nothing more for him to see. He flew back to London on the Monday and filed his report. This time authority, not always noted for the speed of its operations, acted quickly. Very quickly indeed. But not before Peel was in for another incident.

17

One Way Out

On the morning of Monday, 29 September 1941, an Army officer was walking up a narrow footpath opposite the top end of the Peveril Camp. He was close to the guardroom when he stopped. He had suddenly felt his foot sink slightly, as though the ground he had trodden on was hollow underneath. He prodded and discovered that a sod of tangled grass about 1½ feet square had been cut and replaced. It covered a hole about four feet deep with a short ladder running up from its base to the ground-level. The grass was held in place by a light trapdoor.

At once the search was on. It was soon established that there was a tunnel about twenty-five yards long. It led from house No. 13 inside the compound, on the main Peel to Kirk Michael coast road, which formed the camp's inland boundary. Its address is now 17 Peveril Road, known years ago as Ballarat Road. On raising the linoleum on the floor of the small front room, searchers discovered that three of the floorboards had been cut across. When these were lifted, they found a shaft about ten feet deep and four feet across, with a home-made ladder in position going down to the base. There a tunnel headed eastwards, passing out from under the house. It then ran under the perimeter wire and the Peveril Road, sloping upwards and then rose vertically to surface in the middle of a narrow path running between the barbed wire around the outside guardroom on the opposite side of the road, and the hedge of a bungalow owned by R. B. Kelly.

In its report the *Mona's Herald* paid grudging tribute to the tunnel's architects. The line, it said, must have been calculated with the greatest accuracy. An error to the right would have meant surfacing inside the wire round the guardroom, while a foot to the left would have meant coming out in Mr Kelly's garden. The builders must have known they took a great risk in coming up so close to the guardroom. In view of the distance they probably had no alternative.

The tunnel itself was mainly a little over three feet in height. A man could just get along it in the greatest discomfort but without having to crawl snake-like on his belly. It mostly ran through a subsoil of sand and clay, and to prevent its collapsing, the sides and roof had been timbered at intervals. An electric light had been installed roughly half-way along the tunnel. The mains had been tapped in the house, and wires had been run out down the shaft and along to the light point.

From the start the builders had a major problem: the disposal of the clay as they dug it out. They solved this simply but laboriously. The garden of the house in which the tunnel started had been largely made over to growing vegetables. The tunnellers carried off everything they dug, took it through the house to the garden and added it to the vegetable area; the subsoil was later found mixed with the loam, raising the allotment over the level of the surrounding ground. The operation must have taken months, with several men involved.

The Manx police were quickly at work. It was simple to find out from whence the tunnel had been leading. The house was photographed on very simple equipment and was examined in every detail by a team led by the late Inspector Kneen, the men who had taken the escapees from the RN patrol boat which had picked them up little more than a week earlier. The officers even examined the soil on the allotment. They had found the hole below the ground floor with no trouble.

Suspicion was directed at three men who had been living in the house, and they were cross-examined at length. No charges were made; in a camp where everyone had a good reason to want to break out, there were more than 650 potential collaborators in an escape plot. One point was never heavily emphasized and has been disputed, but it is believed by many: the three men who had escaped from Peveril and were later picked up at sea had lived in the house where the operation started.

The tunnel did not last long. It became waterlogged; perhaps it had never been used for the purpose for which it was built; perhaps it had. It was being ruined by seepage even as it was discovered, yet it achieved a wide notoriety as the first tunnel to freedom to be built so painstakingly in a camp in Britain.

The present owners of the house, Gordon Keith and his wife, rediscovered the entrance to the tunnel some years ago when they were stripping out and preparing to relay the flooring and virtually rebuilding the inside of the property. The joists were found to have been cut near the window, and a cover fitted over them. The vertical shaft down to the tunnel could be examined by torchlight, and an attempt was made to get down and along it. The tunnel had, of course, caved in with the years, but at the base of the shaft Mr Keith found a clay pipe, some naval buttons and a spirit level. He started making inquiries, and Peel veterans assured him that they had heard of the tunnel back in 1941, and alleged that among the detainees was an Italian opera singer who 'sang his heart out' to cover the noise of the digging going on below street level. Maybe; maybe not.

The house has been considerably altered, but stone gateposts are still in position, and the irons on which the original gates were hung remain. The garden has also been changed around but it still contains one remarkable link with the past. In the thin soil that raises the level of a turf-topped bank can still be seen pieces of clay tunnelled out from the escape route. Even after forty years it still refuses to mix fully with the flinty earth of the topsoil, and its colour is distinct.

The events of that late September were a welcome diversion to the media. Peel became large in the national news. Reporters were not reluctant to get the Isle of Man assignment. It was a pleasant break, and they made the most of it. Each new occurrence made its headlines; the comings and goings of men such as the Chief Constable were eagerly reported. Manx officials were pursued for interviews. Views were sought on anything about internment camps.

The camp administration came in for some heavy *flak*, aimed more at the higher authority for its allegedly lenient policy than at the men on the spot. The handling of the riot situation on the Saturday night, when a member of the British Government narrowly escaped rough treatment from Fascists and later accepted deputations from the spokesmen for the miscreants, was strongly criticized.

The *Daily Mail* suddenly felt inspired by Kipling's 'If' and excelled itself with some verse entitled *How to Treat A Fascist*. The war was on; the bombs were falling; it was right and proper to overlook its very different attitude to the British Fascist movement during a campaign in the pre-war years:

How to Treat a Fascist

If you can hate your land while others love it,
We'll send you to a camp beside the sea,
No hostile bombers ever roar above it,
You'll get your rations just the same as we.

If you can fill a rather boring minute
By throwing bricks and bottles at the guard,
Though we've a cell we will not put you in it—
We would not dream of treating you too hard.

If others slave, if others die for freedom,
Why should you care, since you are freedom's foe,
Voice your complaints, dear boys, and we will heed them,
Your comfort is our only thought, you know.

If you'll stay here, where there is none to hurt you,
Till we achieve our aim and war is done
We shall not fail to recognise such virtue
And you shall share what better men have won.

On the Monday when the tunnel was discovered, a secondary story also emerged from the Peveril Camp. All the men's camps on the island had a system of token paper money, which had value in the camp only and which was issued to inmates against their accounts in the camp books. These notes were printed locally and were in various modest denominations. Then, on the morning when Sam Ogden was flying back to London with his report in his mind and when unknown to him the hole in the ground was about to be discovered, an auditor reported that unauthorized notes were circulating at Peel. There were examples of a note for a halfpenny having the '½d.' rubbed out and a useful '5s.' substituted; not the easiest thing to do with anything approaching a realistic result, one would imagine.

One printed report suggested that hundreds of pounds were

involved. Fact subsequently revealed that the amount of the swindle amounted to about £3. But it was a good story while it lasted.

The next sitting of Tynwald embarked on a hearty condemnation of the whole administration and conduct of the military in charge of the camps. At times it was not so much a debate as a vigorous slanging match, reflecting the Manx concern. The point generally seized on was the food served inside the barbed wire. Members of the venerable House of Keys took the emphatic view that the internees and detainees should do no better than the man in the street.

Immediately after the Peel riot one privilege was abruptly stopped. Visits by wives were suspended for a month, and only one parcel was allowed weekly; its value was not to exceed 10s. (50p.), and a sales chit giving the amount had to accompany the parcel.

Herbert Morrison, the Home Secretary, the Cockney whose quiff was made famous in the cartoons of David Low, gave significant news to the House of Commons a few days after the riot. He assured Members that, after the Manx courts had disposed of the charges against the three men who had escaped and been recaptured, he proposed to transfer them to a mainland prison where they would be held under close supervision. In reply to a further question asking if it was true that many thousands of bottles of beer were allowed into the camp and whether detainees could drink as much as they wanted, he answered: 'No. They don't get as much beer as they please. I don't think anyone does these days.'

No doubt he was technically right. But the quantity consumed was very high, as the Manx police could doubtless have told him.

With Ogden's return to London events moved rapidly. The day after his visit to the island it was known that widespread changes were to be made in the administration at Peel. On the last day of September the *Mona's Herald* announced that fifty picked Metropolitan policemen would be coming over the following day to act as wardens at the camp. Billets in the town were already being found for them.

What the newspaper did not say was that Ogden, promoted from Chief Inspector to Superintendent for the heavy responsibility, was in overall charge. Over from London on the Saturday; work all week-end; back to headquarters on the Monday;

decisions taken, and back again with a police party under his command on the Wednesday. It was fast going.

Even before the police arrived, the Isle of Man Government had commandeered the Creg Malin, the gaunt pub-cum-hotel next door to the coiled wire of the camp. Huts were quickly put up along a narrow lane behind it and were used for stores or for interview rooms for visitors.

Once more Herbert Morrison was able to tell the House of Commons what was going on. The accounts of the disorder, he maintained, had been exaggerated, and he reminded the House that 'these men were detained for preventative, not punitive, purposes'. But it was necessary to restore discipline in the camp so he had decided to reinforce the military with a detachment of the Metropolitan Police which had been specially picked for the work.

While the Home Secretary was making his statement in London, eighteen men who were considered the ringleaders of the trouble had been taken from Peveril to the main prison in Douglas. The following morning they were driven off in a military lorry and placed on the Liverpool steamer. They were guarded by an escort of Metropolitan PCs. Their destination was Walton Gaol, where they arrived that afternoon. They left behind them in the Douglas gaol the three men awaiting their trial by the Manx courts.

The arrival of the men from the Met was welcomed by the Manx. These men knew the Fascists and the terrorists from the streets of London. There would be no more nonsense. The Manx newspapers insisted that there was now a real prospect of the Fascist detainees being kept in their proper place, 'and the inhabitants of the town and island have been given security for their lives and property'. The new Superintendent was described as an unassuming man who in his young days had been no mean boxer. The Manx public were treated to the news that when he found time he was partial to a round of golf. He seems to have had a quiet sense of humour, and certainly a sense of occasion.

It had been arranged with the landlord that the police would formally occupy the Creg Malin from Saturday night and would take over their duties at the camp at noon on Monday. Proprietor Ostick had been ordered to get out along with his guests by closing time on Saturday. The catering and general supervision of the place were to go to John Kelly, of Douglas, an ex-chief steward of the Steam Packet line. Accordingly, at the normal closing time on Saturday night, Sam Ogden went behind the bar in the main lounge of the Creg Malin and called a one-word order of command: 'Time.'

At noon on Monday the Metropolitan Police duly took over the main duties of the camp, with the military acting as perimeter guards. The line of responsibility was clearly laid down. Ogden was the man in charge, with Divisional Inspector Frank Mulvey as his deputy. The people of Peel were well pleased.

A few days later they read how the Home Secretary had announced that, as a punishment, the detainees in the Peel camp had been barred from going to the cinema for a month. There was only one cinema in Peel. Its owner, Ostick, had very pronounced views about detainees, who with their womenfolk constituted a nuisance to him. He disliked them heartily and would not allow them into his cinema until much later in the war.

At the end of October the wives of the Peel detainees were once again allowed supervised visits to their husbands; a reception hut had been put aside for the purpose behind the Creg Malin, a yard or two from the camp.

In the early days a liberal number of visits had been allowed; there was one woman who lived in the West Country on the mainland and who made the tortuous journey to London, to Liverpool and then to Douglas, to see her man every fortnight. There were even four wives who had taken up lodgings in Peel, to save themselves the journey.

Steadily the rules were tightened. The number of permitted visits was cut down. Late in November Peel was declared a Protected Area under the Defence Regulations. This meant that only residents and authorized people had an automatic right to be there; anyone with Home Office permission to visit the camp could remain only for the stipulated period of the visit and if staying overnight could not lodge in the small town; British subjects, other than residents and those connected with the camp, could enter only when allowed by the Chief Constable. No barriers were erected on the approaches to the town, but spot checks were made from time to time, and the wise man carried his identity card.

Only a few days before the new restrictions started at Peel, the three escapees made their final appearance before the Manx court, answering the charge of stealing a fishing-boat and two

sets of oars. One of them was additionally charged with unlaw-
fully altering an entry on his identity card.

The cases permitted of little argument. Perhaps the most
significant remark was made by the Attorney General in his
opening speech for the prosecution. Describing the chain of
events, he referred to the way the men, on being landed from the
naval craft, were taken back to Peveril—'this ill-judged action', as
he called it. This senior member of the Manx Bar was puzzled
why authority ordered that such men should be returned to camp
instead of putting them straight into police custody; It was a
decision whose consequences earned some hard criticism.

The case itself was soon disposed of. The trio received
sentences varying from six months to one year. By then there had
been yet another attempted escape from another Manx camp,
this one more spectacular.

18

A Long Way Round

In only one other escape attempt did men succeed in getting off
the Isle of Man, and then their stormy journey ended in failure.
They too were a trio, but they were of a very different calibre from
the three who had put to sea from Castletown. Intelligent men,
consisting of two ship's officers from the Dutch mercantile
marine, and a Dutch civilian air pilot, they were pro-Nazi, and
they escaped from Mooragh Camp, Ramsey, on the night of
Wednesday 15 October 1941. Details of their escape from Ramsey
are conflicting, and it is probable that the most accurate account
was provided by an acting sergeant in the CID of the Manx police
who later accompanied them back to camp and had ample opportunity to get at the facts.

The report of the case lists them as having escaped from camp
sometime between six o'clock on the Wednesday evening, when
they were present at the rollcall, and nine on the Thursday
morning, when they were found to be missing and the alarm was
immediately raised. In reality they had escaped at about half-past
nine at night.

They admitted to the police sergeant that they had planned to
get out for about two months, and they had certainly planned
carefully. Then abruptly they learned that on the Thursday they
were to be transferred to Peveril Camp. They disliked this idea,
and escape during the Wednesday night became imperative,
regardless of weather conditions.

They had built themselves a ladder with which they could climb to the top of the barbed wire. They had also lashed together two lengths of wood long enough to make a crude bridge across the top of the two lines of wire, from which they could then jump down to freedom. They had it all worked out; they even studied Ramsey Harbour during their official exercise walks and had spotted the yacht *Irene* and made a mental note of the position of a rowing-boat they could use to get out to her.

The plan went wrong, but this did not prevent the escape attempt. The ladder, which had been hidden in a lavatory, had disappeared. It had doubtless been found by the military and removed. This meant that they could no longer hope to climb up and over the wire. The men, however, had time to acquire a pair of pliers. They had already kept careful watch on the movements of the guards and knew the time between their appearances at a key point. They also noticed how the guards tended to take shelter in their huts on rainy nights, extending the interval between patrols.

The night of the 15th was a bad one, with a Force 10 gale, and the trio realized that the weather was against them. The prospect of a move to Peveril decided things. They cut the wire at grass level and were through.

Within ten minutes of escaping they were on board the yacht *Irene*. They later told the police that they distantly remembered hearing the noisy departure of men leaving a pub near the other side of the Swing Bridge. This suggests that it was about closing time, ten o'clock. The trio had armed themselves with a wooden pole from the camp. It enabled them to steer the small rowing-boat across the harbour to the yacht. They then cut the mooring ropes and left the dinghy tied up in place of the yacht.

The *Irene* had been correctly immobilized, but the tide was ebbing. Just as they had used their pole to steer across the harbour, so they used it to get the yacht clear to the sea, setting the sails as they did so. The rest must have been a nightmare, particularly for the air pilot. But off they steered for Ireland.

The Irish Sea in late September had been much too much for the three detainees who had escaped from Peel. Even though the Dutch trio included two experienced sailors, they were helpless in a powerless yacht when that same sea was running one of its autumnal storms with a south-westerly gale.

There is a strong implication that the British services played a cat-and-mouse game in what subsequently happened. As soon as the alarm was raised, a motor launch with an armed crew and police put to sea, and RAF aircraft combined with three naval patrol vessels from the island in a systematic sea search. The escape alarm system had worked with great thoroughness; boats were searched before leaving the island, just in case the trio had put back to shore and somehow made their way on to a passenger ship or a fishing-boat. The port authorities were alerted at Fleetwood and arrangements made to comb through the Steam Packet's vessel as soon as it arrived there from Douglas.

A massive search was carried out on the island. The Home Guard, special constables, scouts, sea scouts, cadets and police themselves all combined in one operation, while coastguards and port authorities kept special watch. Airfields and military installations had been advised, and the whole elaborate alert system was in operation.

Visibility was bad; the seas were described as 'mountainous'. The chance that an incapacitated yacht could cross westwards was virtually nil, especially considering the condition of the crew, without food, without proper shelter and without warmth. Precisely when they were spotted is uncertain; such details as remain are ambiguous. 'The following day' could have been the day after the men were last known to be in camp, or the day after they were declared missing. It could have been Thursday or Friday. At any rate, the RAF from a local station sighted the yacht and reported her.

No attempt was made to board her. The mouse was trapped; the cat may have been at play. The position of the yacht was precisely known, as were the conditions of the sea. The fact that she was helpless against the westerlies was obvious. It was only necessary to keep an eye on her. It was approaching midnight on Saturday when the Ramsey yacht, outward bound for Ireland, grounded on a small creek near Eskmeals, south of St Bees Head on the coast of Cumberland. The three men from Mooragh scrambled ashore, exhausted and ravenous, their clothing saturated. They were soon arrested, which, considering the lateness of the hour and the sparseness of the area, suggested that they had been watched for some time. The yacht was undamaged and later returned to the Isle of Man.

They were allowed to change into dry battledress and were taken to Whitehaven under military guard and handed over to the police. A Manx police escort arrived on the first boat and took them back to Douglas. The established procedure then followed. The trio were taken back to Ramsey and returned to camp. They were then arrested after the paperwork was completed, and charged with stealing the yacht *Irene* valued at £300. In their statements it turned out that their intention was to contact the German Consul in Dublin in the hope that he could arrange their return to Holland. They seemed proud of their escapade, claimed to have laid their plans well and were convinced that they were foiled only by the fierce storms. They seem not to have realized that their westward journey had covered roughly thirty-five miles eastwards at half a knot.

At their trial they pleaded Not Guilty to stealing the boat, saying that they had merely borrowed it to travel to a neutral country. They intended to arrange through the German Consulate in Dublin that the Irish authorities would return the boat to the owner or advise him where it was to be found.

The Manx police revealed that when arrested one of the men, not the air pilot, was found to possess a sketch map, in ink, of the Isle of Man and the east coast of Ireland, with some appropriate nautical details.

Despite their plea of innocence, the men each received six months' prison sentences. They were graded as Second Class Offenders in the Manx gaol, which meant that they had never previously been convicted and were subject to the prison's ordinary rules but had a more varied and liberal diet than citizens in the third class.

After serving their sentences they were released and were returned not to Mooragh Camp but to Peveril in Peel, to avoid which transfer they had timed their escape all those months ago. It had taken them quite a time to get there.

19

The Ladies of Laxey

By the end of 1941 and the early days of the following year the internment camps on the Isle of Man had been steadily thinned out and their composition had changed. Away in Rushen there were now barely a thousand internees divided between the main women's camp in Port Erin and the married camp in Port St Mary, and one in every four of them was to be released by the end of 1942.

The alteration in the make-up of the men's camps occurred in the last weeks of the year, actually increasing their population for a brief time. This was due to the spread of war and to the number of countries that had been persuaded or bullied into signing with the Axis. Thus in the middle of December 1941 400 nationals of such countries were brought over to the island; they included Japanese, Hungarians, Romanians and a disproportionate number of Finns, most of whom were merchant seamen.

They were housed in Palace, in Douglas, which had previously held Italians and which had been emptied some weeks earlier to prepare for a new and mixed bag of arrivals. The various nationalities were segregated inside the camp, which was sectionalized to keep them apart. By the end of February the number of these nationals was 573, of whom 340 were Finns and 90 Japanese. It was in all a sizeable proportion of the whole number, for on 28 February 1942 the total male internment figure was 3,052, to which must be added the 496 detainees left in Peveril. Exactly a year earlier the total had been 5,690.

The earlier Japanese arrivals—34 of them—were described by a Manx newspaper with something approaching respect. They were by far the most prosperous-looking members of the incoming contingent, many of them 'having the appearance of well-to-do business men'. The reportage was accurate, for that is precisely what they were. They came from the very small but flourishing Japanese business community in the city of London, and most of them were seniors in the London branch of a Yokohama bank. It was believed that their top director was a member of the Japanese imperial family. Whether that was true or not, he was immediately made leader of the house which had been assigned to the party in the Palace Camp, and no unit in any of the camps was said to approach it for severe cleanliness. The main staircase had been scrubbed white by the first morning after their arrival, and the place was run on strict military lines. The same reporter wrote sniffily that the next consignment of Japs was very different. Yet, even so, the Japanese were the star internees.

In all it had been a strange Christmas on the island. Much fuss was made of a reunion party for blitzed babies from Merseyside which was held at Douglas Town Hall. An Italian internee at Onchan chose the season to leap to death from a top-floor window, having made previous attempts to commit suicide. A party with a visit from Santa Claus was the main feature of improvised jollity in the married camp; but the Manx themselves were not too happy. Turkeys were hard to come by and geese were scarce. The messing officers of the military establishments had been going round with order books at the ready. It was a strange Christmas.

It was symptomatic of the times, too, that the first news of releases among the Japanese internees referred not to the business men but to a few who had arrived in Douglas some weeks later. They were experts at chicken sexing, a craft at which the Japanese were widely thought to have an almost mystical skill. It meant the ability to determine the sex of day-old chicks and in those days was considered to be highly specialized. Strong representations for their release had been made by the remnants of the poultry industry. The skill of these men was needed urgently.

A number of distinguished visitors came to the island during the year. Chief among them was Herbert Morrison, the cheerful Home Secretary, who was no harsh disciplinarian; he came for Tynwald Day, a gesture much appreciated by the Manx, and stayed on to inspect the camps, for which he held the ultimate responsibility. Holiday visitors were a mere trickle compared with normal times. However, the Manx were very pleased by the presence of the police from the blitzed areas of northern England. The first of them had reached the island back in August 1941, some with their wives; their duties were confined to the Peel and Port St Mary areas. To them this was almost a holiday.

The number of police from the blitzed areas of Lancashire was never more than a small token force, and even this produced a mass of paperwork arguing about their messing allowance. The original grant to the individual constable had been 8s. 6d. (42½p.) per day, but soon after New Year's Day in 1942 London asked if this figure could be reduced. It was; the Manx police had to report that inquiries showed that the landladies at the billets were receiving 6s. 6d. (32½p.) a day, which implied that the visiting constables were making a basic profit. At any rate another inquiry was started in January, and London solemnly decreed that the rate from February onwards would be reduced from 8s. 6d. (42½p.) a day to 7s. (35p.).

Meanwhile the war went on.

In March the Chief Constable continued examining his problems of staff shortage. Police were needed in the south-west of the island, in Port St Mary and Port Erin, where no soldiers guarded the camps and the load on the police was a heavy one. A census revealed that on 20 March there were fifteen male auxiliary constables at Port Erin and fourteen at Port St Mary, all on camp duties. At Peel there were seven. Mainland police, apart from the London men on special duties at Peveril, were down to one sergeant and six constables at Peel, and four constables at Port St Mary. At Port Erin there were six policewomen and one sergeant all from London. Then the call-up bit into the numbers of the regular police all over the realm, and men simply could not be spared to go to the Isle of Man. All this produced an extraordinary battle by typewriter, with the memoranda going backwards and forwards rather in the manner of a ceaseless rally at tennis. The object of the game was for London to ensure that imperial funds were not spent paying for police work that was

17 Peveril Road, Peel, after modernizing. Even its number and the name of the road itself have changed. The escape tunnel from the camp was dug from the front room and surfaced in the narrow path shown in the foreground

The right-hand post and iron hinge of the gate at 17 Peveril Road, Peel, are the same today (*left*) as they were then, when barbed wire spread out in front of the house (*below*). The guardhouse can be seen (*below right*); the picture was taken following the discovery of the tunnel which came out in the narrow path, still there today. The guardhouse has been moved a mile along the road

Original photographs taken from inside the front room of 17 Peveril Road on the discovery of the escape tunnel from the Peveril Camp on 29 September 1941. The shoring-up of the walls and the running of an electric light cable are clearly shown (*above*). The cutting of the joists under the ground floor and the ten-foot descent into the tunnel are seen in the lower picture

Forged US naval passes found on two internees who were caught in an escape attempt from Peveril Camp, Peel. 'Haggit' tried to tear up his 'pass' when arrested

part of the normal duties of the island force. The return of service, as it were, was to ensure that the island was recompensed where the extra work could not be held to be solely Manx. An example was the payment for the male auxiliary constables—men enlisted in place of constables taken for the fighting forces. Such men were vital for camp duties in Rushen. The question of who finally paid for them was a bureaucratic delight. At one time London seemed to be paying for one-half of a Manx policeman and local government funds for the other.

The problems eased somewhat in August 1942 when Commandant Cuthbert decided to move his married camp from Port St Mary to the northern end of Port Erin, known locally as Spaldrick. This was made possible by the steadily declining number of women in the main camp; by rearranging accommodation, the small Spaldrick area could be released for the marrieds, moving the women who were still there to houses to the south of Port Erin and so freeing the Port St Mary village completely. It would cease to be a restricted area.

The work of moving camp took little more than a day. Husbands worked away at the cheerful job of loading lorries with baggage and unloading it in the new quarters. The pro-Nazi couples were put up mainly at the Towers, and the Italians at the Waverley. Couples of other nationalities and the uncommitted were allocated to the various houses in the small area. The two camps remained in their new form to the end of the war, separated from each other by a wire fence. Even the landladies gave a hand to help the removal operation. But to help the Commandant those landladies were prepared to do most things. To them he was a highly popular figure: he had won them over. Some of them convinced themselves that he had once been an actor. His talks the previous year about the precautions that would be taken before the married camp opened had been very well received. Although he may never have realized it, this peacetime policeman had many friends and supporters: to the internee women he was a fair-minded man who commanded respect. It was a tribute to him that Germans who had first seen him at a tribunal at Bow Street took a similar view.

At about the same time in 1942 preparations of an entirely different sort were taking shape on the opposite side of the island, at Laxey, a hilly village that descended steeply to the sea. It was a place of much charm, except perhaps in the easterlies, when the air bites shrewdly.

Laxey had been selected as the village where the women and children from Madagascar were to be quartered. They were not internees and certainly not to be regarded as such. They were the victims of the sad business between the British and the French that had followed the capitulation of one part of France. The British had made a successful landing on Madagascar, which was French territory controlled across thousands of miles by the authorities in Vichy, which had officially surrendered to the Germans, who could thus use French possessions overseas. The local French forces resisted the British landing: there was fighting; there were casualties; there were losses. The British collected a mixed bag of men, mostly officers, from the garrison and the naval forces and some civilians, and packed them off to Scotland. They were not prisoners of war, but they had to be classified; their position was complex, the result of a complex war scene.

The men, some with wives and families, finally docked at Glasgow. They went on to various camps in the north of England, usually to Grizedale in Westmorland, while they made up their minds whether they wanted to throw in their lot with the Free French, through the de Gaulle headquarters in Carlton House Terrace, London. The women and children were gathered together while plans were made for them to be sent across to Laxey. There they were to await the decision by their husbands to fight with the Allies or not. By early September about sixty women and children had reached the island and were billeted in private guest-houses, almost all of them in Laxey, a few in the even smaller hamlet of Baldrine, which was next to it along the coast road. Sixty-four names had been supplied to the island in advance by the authorities, including that of Madame Lucienne Claerebout, wife of General Claerebout who had so recently commanded the defence of Diego Suarez against the British. The women arrived to be put in the care of Norah J. Banks of the Home Office, who was working in the women's camp at Port Erin and had been sent across to Laxey in advance to fix billets. At all times the dictum went out: these women are not internees. They were to live in Laxey; they would have as much freedom as any other alien except that there would be a three-mile boundary restriction on their movements. Women must have separate beds in billets, but children could share a double bed where necessary. Landladies would receive a guinea (£1.05p.) a week for each adult billeted on them, and 15s. (75p.) per child. The new arrivals would be subject to curfew.

The women were essentially colonials; they lived wherever their husbands were posted by the force or department to which they were attached. Many of them had forgotten what it meant to have a permanent home; they were used to service accommodation and the minor grumbles attached to such postings. And Laxey, as September evenings drew in, hardly rivalled tropical Madagascar. They were lonely, and their feelings were decidedly mixed.

The day after they arrived, they were photographed and issued with official papers establishing their address in Laxey. In all they occupied ten houses, at six or more to a house. An interpreter was provided for them at the local post office. Miss Banks was at the village commissioner's office to help and handle complaints, if any.

These did not take long to arrive. Reportage on this point differs very sharply. According to Miss Banks, who seems to have been a very thorough and conscientious official, the women were not in the least anti-British, despite what had happened, and many of them professed the friendliest feelings. One or two, she said, were nurses, married to doctors, and both they and their husbands had done fine work for British servicemen wounded in the operations in Madagascar. By the end of the first week in Laxey most of the women were wearing badges bearing the triskele, the Three Legs of Man. These they had bought at the start of their shopping expeditions. They were Roman Catholics, and it was arranged that Mass would be celebrated in the Pavilion of Laxey Glen Gardens, the priest being Father James McGrath, from Onchan. The temperature was the great problem; coming from a hot climate, the women found the Isle of Man decidedly bleak; the painstaking Miss Banks duly asked the landladies to provide good fires when the weather became colder.

So on the surface all was in reasonably good order, but the private eye of military officialdom thought it knew better. The ladies had not been in Laxey for a week before an experienced observer reported back to his chief in Douglas. Of the ten billets in use, he said, four were without bathrooms, and more suitable billets were being found. He obviously thought that Miss Banks, whom he plainly respected, was being optimistic when she said that the Frenchwomen were reasonably satisfied. He went far beyond this and alleged that a well-connected woman from the mainland, a naturalized British subject, who had taken a room in a local hotel, was 'adopting' the French women. She had even found what she considered a more suitable place for them in a large hotel north of Ramsey, where she had worked out suitable terms with the owners; it was near a security area, and the Manx authorities would certainly have forbidden any such move on security grounds. The woman had important contacts in London; she seemed determined to come to the aid of the French. However, reported the observer, she was souring the minds of the Frenchwomen against Miss Banks, whom she wanted to get replaced anyway.

Such was the feeling on 9 September 1942, less than a week after the women had arrived in Laxey.

Three days later the visitor was served with a notice signed by the Lieutenant Governor requiring her to leave the area to which the French nationals were restricted. She obeyed, reluctantly.

A number of Frenchmen, mainly serving officers, arrived to join their wives and families; most of them reached Laxey in the middle of November, some arrived on Christmas Eve, and in all there were then approaching a hundred French nationals in the village. Most conspicuous among them all was General Claerebout himself, striding along in the Douglas shopping area with his wife and children in his wake, enjoying the regular shopping expeditions which the Laxey party was given by official permit, usually accompanied by the energetic Miss Banks. Several of the French Army men, having decided on their future allegiance, went off to London and to the Free French forces. Some had been on the island for only a week or two. They were the advance guard. The rest of the Laxey French were to follow them.

The main exodus was on 18 January, when a party of sixty-eight women and children was taken to the mainland under the wing of Miss Banks, who remained with them until they left Britain, mostly for northern Africa and in some cases Zanzibar. Elaborate arrangements had to be made by the Manx Government Office for their trip to the mainland. The departure went off without incident, and two of the French wives were known to inquire later if they could return to Laxey if accommodation could be found for them. Their husbands, who had never been on the island, had joined de Gaulle and were away on service, and the wives found themselves thinking back favourably on the picturesque village on the Manx escarpment.

One French family stayed behind. The wife was expecting her third child. The local authorities gave their permission, and she and her husband moved to Douglas to be near the island's maternity home; they did not leave until some months later.

With the departure of the party, down came the notices in French that had been posted on the roads leading in and out of Laxey to mark the three-mile limit beyond which the newcomers could not go without a permit. They had been put up at the request of the diligent Miss Banks.

Once the women were outward bound from Britain, most of them heading for Africa and a warmer climate, Miss Banks returned to the island, having seen them off. She was able to write: 'Laxey seems very lonely now without the chattering French people, who were really sorry to go and have left with nothing but pleasant memories of their treatment in Laxey.'

Norah Banks had been proved right. There had been rumours of spirited slanging matches between landladies and visitors, of complaints on both sides, of attempts to take the dissatisfaction to the higher levels of the Foreign Office and even the floor of the House of Commons. The alarmists were proved wrong. The last word was said by the quiet Miss Banks, believed not to have been a professional civil servant but a schoolteacher doing welfare work as her contribution to the war effort. Her job over, she went back to Port Erin and carried on at her normal post.

If he had not had toothache, Giovanni Moneta would probably have stayed in the Metropole Camp for the rest of the war and then been shipped back to Italy. As a merchant seaman he would not be released until peace arrived. But toothache he had, and with it the pattern of his life changed completely.

He saw the camp dentist and had a normal and purely routine extraction. There was no reason to suspect any real trouble. But Giovanni did not heal; not long after the extraction he had a haemorrhage. Surprised, for such a thing had never happened to him before, he reported to the camp doctor. This was not a case for surgery, nor could he remain a long time in the camp sick-bay.

He could have been sent up the hill to Falcon Cliff, or he could be sent to Ballaquane, the small unit that had been organized inside the wire at Peveril across at Peel. He was lucky; he was sent to Ballaquane. He then found himself under the RAMC Commanding Officer, Lieutenant-Colonel R. Flowerdew, who had spent his service with the Indian Army, an internee assistant doctor named Altmann, who came from London, and two women, an English matron and a Manx nursing sister named Margaret Cannell.

Moneta mended slowly. The time came when he would be sent back to Metropole and farm work. But Ballaquane needed another orderly. He volunteered for the job and was very glad to get it. He stayed there for most of his remaining time on the Isle of Man. His main duty was to total up the various food requirements that had been prescribed for the different patients, to get the list signed by the matron and then collect the various rations from the food stores. At different times he found himself dealing with the diet sheets of a Japanese, an Austrian baron, a Spanish toreador, a member of the French Foreign Legion and the occasional European Jew who might require a kosher version of the hospital diet.

Moneta settled to his new life of internment. He was no longer on farm work, although Peel detainees did in some cases go out on farm parties under escort. Instead there were ample walks and plenty of time for hobbies, which the authorities encouraged. He took up art and still has some of his paintings. Other inmates of the small hospital busied themselves with the traditional pastimes of the war prisoner—model ships that could be inserted and positioned in bottles; belts; shopping baskets and the like; woodwork, particularly making chess sets, was also very popular.

Moneta liked his new life and thought it an improvement on Metropole. He also liked Margaret Cannell.

20

A Case of Murder?

Palace Camp had closed in November 1942 and was never to be reopened as an internment centre. When it wound up, it consisted of about 260 Finns, some of whom were released altogether, while the bulk of them—180 at the first count—were moved up to Mooragh. So 1943 had opened with a total of just under 2,990 men held in all on the island whereas it had been roughly 3,700 a year earlier. And by 1 January 1944 the total had fallen to 2,068. Internment was down mainly to the hard core.

These totals fluctuated week by week, almost day by day but departures predominated. Occasionally the number was augmented by an intake of internees who had been sent to Canada and were now coming back to be released but were held temporarily in the Isle of Man while the paperwork ran its course. It all made arduous desk work for the distant men with the shiny elbows. No war, except possibly the next, can be won without them.

The Finns who had moved on from Palace to Mooragh settled into two factions, the pro-Nazi and the pro-British. Those friendly to Britain were thought to be in the minority, but the two lots were not kept apart, except from the other nationals in the Mooragh camp. The men were nearly all merchant seamen; most were from below decks. They were mainly an ill-educated lot, a very different type of internee from the academics at Hutchinson in the early days. Some had been interned since the previous year, and those who were willing to work for the Allied cause had been steadily released. This meant that the pro-Nazi element which remained behind dominated the Finns more and more. It was not difficult for them to make contact through the wire with the German Nazis in another section of the camp, and the bullying and bluster increased steadily.

By the beginning of April 1943 the Finns at Mooragh numbered 140, about a quarter of the camp's total population, consisting otherwise mostly of Germans and Italians. At the end of April the number was 141. This did not mean that there was a newcomer. It meant that there had been two newcomers during the month.

For shortly after midday on 20 April one of the Finns was killed.

How he died was not in doubt. He was stabbed in the chest; the knife penetrated his heart and he died almost at once. Why he was murdered, and if the stabbing even constituted murder, is another matter; most of the trial that followed was held *in camera* as things considered secret at the time had to be considered by the jury. These consisted mostly of details of conditions inside the camp. They were very relevant to the trial, and they would have made startling general reading in April 1943.

Relations, as far as there were any, between Britain and Finland at that stage of the war were delicate; the Finns had declared for the Germans because they hated Russia, not because they had any particular quarrel with the western powers. Many Finns, as had already been proved by the movement of a number of them into the services and war work, were pro-British. There was no sense therefore in holding a trial in open court when a killing might have a political significance; any disclosures might not lengthen the war by five minutes, but the matter called for discretion.

It was not unknown to the people of Ramsey that there was trouble inside the camp, although they knew no details. The noise of quarrelling reached the world outside the wire. Finns of this sort were tough customers. They were often homeless men, semi-literate and semi-vagabond; in peace they divided their time between the forecastle, the bar and the brothel. They drank not for pleasure but for oblivion. They fought. Their standards were different from those of western Europeans. There was no Sibelius among them. They lived roughly and dangerously.

In an internment camp all this was clamped down only for the anger within the men to rise to bursting-point. They would be searched, and there was no question of knife-carrying, thus denying them what they regarded as a symbol of virility and preparedness. But the Finns were a boisterous, hearty lot. They possessed a vast energy, and they had to get rid of it. In their first camp as well as in Mooragh they had rigged up a rough gymnasium for themselves and, according to a Manx doctor who surveyed the scene later, they had even made boxing-gloves of a sort by cutting them out of carpets. Such were the Finns. They could vent their feelings in a clumsy boxing ring. Or they had other ways.

In Mooragh they could spend a little of their camp token money on a beer if they wanted to, a privilege that had been denied them in their last camp. Unknown to the authorities, they had their own means of increasing the alcoholic intake. They were known to boost their booze with an assortment of additives—hair oil, boot-blacking and wood polish among other oddities—and make a highly potent brew. Most dangerous of all, they would pass gas through a harmless ale and emerge with something that could make a man fighting drunk before he passed out. To some extent this sort of thing went on periodically in most of the camps that housed hardliners, but in April that year it was at its worst in the Finnish section at Mooragh.

The week-end before the knifing the noise in the camp increased and plainly sounded the mounting unrest. The Nazi element was in full cry; Hitler's birthday was anticipated by the looting of the canteen and the theft of all available liquor, which was no doubt tampered with. The result was a widespread hangover in which heads were sore and tempers frayed. Bullying became rampant; Nazi and Fascist songs were loud in the air, and it was said later that men lolled about clutching bottles of drink, many of them drunk and semi-conscious. The braggarts were vociferous, and sections of the camp were dangerous places for the minority. The attacks and beatings-up increased over the week-end. Fist fights became frequent, and there were many brawls.

But a knifing, leaving a man dying in the road, was unique. It had never happened before in any of the camps, while thousands of men had passed in and out of the wire.

Thus it came about that, on 15 June 1943 in the Court of General Gaol in Douglas, a Finn aged thirty-six was charged with the murder of a fellow Finn, aged twenty-six. The incident on which the charge was based had taken place shortly after noon on 20 April.

The trial was to last nearly a week, a long time in a Manx court in those days. The jurors had been warned that they might be in for a long stay, and they arrived at the Court House with toiletries and a change of clothing, carried in attaché cases, the hand-luggage of those times. In all, seventy-two good men and true had been summoned. The chosen twelve were accommodated in Douglas for the duration of the hearing.

Right at the start the Attorney General applied under the Emergency Powers Defence Act for much of the trial to be heard *in camera*. He said he would have to go fully into matters of a secret nature and he would ask that the Court be cleared.

It was. Vital evidence was given by an internee doctor named Martin Scholtz. His duty was to assist in running the Mooragh Camp hospital. He was the link between the outside Manx doctor who officially looked after the internees and the men themselves. He was to Mooragh what Dr Altmann was to Ballaquane over at Peel, and what Hermann Scholz had been at Hutchinson.

He is believed to have revealed how the camp was sectioned off with wires inside the main perimeter wiring, separating the various nationals into individual units. He explained that he was looking into the adjoining section through the wire separating it from the Germans and saw that the occupants were quiet, walking or sitting in the sun. He said that there had already been three accident cases in the camp that morning. The internees, he said, were normally very quiet people but when excited they would not mind breaking anyone's leg.

At the time he looked through the dividing wire, he saw the now dead man go down the steps of House 8, carrying a bucket in his right hand. He walked hurriedly, and when he reached the pavement, he waved people aside with his left hand. He walked across the pavement until he was opposite to the entrance of House 9. There he raised the bucket and threw the contents over an internee who was standing near the footpath. The bucket contained dirty water, and it was thrown over the man's face. The Finn, now the prisoner, seemed surprised at the attack, looked about him for a second or two and mumbled something.

Then the prisoner went for the deceased, drawing his hand from his right-hand trouser pocket. The other men stepped back a pace or two, the bucket still in his right hand. The doctor said that he saw the prisoner jerk out his hand and give his attacker what appeared to be a knock in the region of the stomach. The man lurched back, swinging his hands wildly. He staggered to the entrance of House 8, then he turned round; his face was pale and he fell on his back without attempting to save himself. When he hit the ground, the doctor could see a great blotch of blood staining the front of his shirt and trousers and he lay quite still. He was stabbed and dying.

Doctor Scholtz hurried to the camp hospital and told the orderlies to collect a stretcher. He also contacted the MO, and they both ran to the gate of the Finnish section of the camp. They heard an uproar and saw a man being attacked and the body of the dead man being pushed on a handcart.

The guard opened the gate to let the handcart through, and at the same time the prisoner ran through the gate and was taken into custody by two of the military guard, who took him to the camp hospital. He would have been killed if he had not been taken out.

Evidence was given earlier in the trial by the Ramsey physician who was official MO to Mooragh. He explained how he saw a man being beaten up by a crowd of aliens. He saw another man being lifted from the ground and placed on a handcart. He examined the man and found he was dead.

The prisoner, who was the man who had been beaten, was examined in the camp hospital, and it was found that his nose was broken; he had severe head injuries and was so badly knocked about that he was only partly conscious. The doctor arranged for him to be moved to Noble's Hospital, where he stayed for some weeks. The doctor said later that he had never seen a man get a worse beating-up than the prisoner had received.

On examining the dead man, the MO found a single wound in the lower part of the chest, about three inches deep, which had penetrated the heart. A post mortem confirmed this evidence. A table knife, with a blade about half the usual length and worn down on both sides, could have caused the wound on the chest wall. Death was caused by one blow only. There was no sign that the dead man had taken drink.

At the end of five days' hearing the jury returned to court after an absence of seventy-five minutes. The prisoner regarded them almost with indifference and sat motionless until the judge, Deemster Cowley, addressed him.

The verdict was: Not Guilty. The accused was also found not

guilty of manslaughter and was discharged and returned to the custody of the internment camp authorities. Two representatives of the Swedish Legation, the Protecting Power for the Finns, were sitting in Court when the verdict was given. They had been on an inspection tour of the camps and had spent some time attending the trial.

The case produced much discussion, particularly on the island. Despite the brevity of the court reports, some details leaked out. In the tiresome catchphrase of those years, there was a war on, and it was felt that war took many shapes. British authority at the time very likely had no desire to see a Finn found guilty of murdering a Finn, with all the consequences of a murder verdict. So ran the gossip. A man was dead; it was better that the matter should be buried, like the victim.

Inevitably, such ideas kindle their own fire. Rumours abounded on the island and took various forms. In the weeks that followed the trial it was even said that important letters had been received from London. This sort of talk was almost certainly nonsense, and there is no record to justify anything of the sort; it could well be that a freer reportage of the trial would have meant less speculation afterwards. Had the public been able to read the spirited defence and the judge's summing up, there would have been less gossip.

The acquittal was not due to any official desire to cover up a killing that had political enmity behind it; credit for the verdict must surely go to the stubborn and painstaking pleading of the defending Manx advocate, R. Kinley Eason, who was many years later to be elevated to the position of one of the island's two Deemsters and who at that time practised in Ramsey. Mr Eason sowed doubt and reaped a brilliant result. He was a jaunty but diminutive man, armed with an array of law books from which he liked to quote learned and complex precedents. A case was a case, and this one had to be won. There could be three final views: the prisoner was guilty of murder, guilty of manslaughter or, if the provocation was such as to justify him in thinking his life was in danger, then he was totally not guilty. So argued the defence, and the legal logic was sound.

Between counsel and client there was a massive divide. They had no language in common. But the defence counsel had the law books, with whose points he made much play. He skilfully widened the area of doubt, until in the mind of the jury it faded altogether. The Finn had been in mortal danger. He had remained almost motionless throughout the trial. He listened apparently attentively to a verdict whose words he could not understand. He betrayed not the slightest emotion when the interpreter translated and repeated them. He did then say two words himself, through the official. 'Thank you.'

Justice had been called for, and justice was done. A man came on trial for his life and was saved by a quite resolute defence, about which little could be said at the time.

And there the matter rested.

21

No Way Out

At the end of the War the Manx authorities were able to say with understandable pride that there had been no permanent escape from the island camps, although there had been many attempts. Six men had managed to get out and put to sea, and three of them had been allowed to reach the mainland, the very last place they wished to be, only to be promptly taken over by the military. The more dangerous trio had been hauled back.

The number of escape attempts, the great majority of which were quite minor incidents, was fifty-seven, of which fifty-six seem to be reasonably documented, the other one having gone unrecorded except for a strongly critical complaint by Chief Constable Young, whose men had found out about it themselves. An escape was listed as such only if a man got out of a camp or if he got away from a working party. Men intercepted at once in the immediate vicinity of the camp did not cause the alarm system to go into operation and were dealt with by the camp authorities. Such cases were not included; the police did not even know of them. The police did, however, very quickly discover the first escape of them all, although it was never the cause of an alert.

The Chief Constable immediately complained to a most important official in distant London. Writing on 21 August 1941, he said that the first escape of an internee had occurred on the night of 17/18 August, when a young Italian cut the wires and got out from Palace. He was discovered by a sentry at the rear of the camp, appeared before the Camp Commander and was given fourteen days' detention. No information had been sent by the camp authorities to the police, who had found out from their own sources.

The Chief Constable considered that the early apprehension of the internee, as he put it, did not alter the gravity of the case, which could well be more serious if it happened again, and the punishment seemed trivial.

The likelihood is that the man heard a sentry approaching and dived for cover in the whins on the cliff behind the camp. The sentry may almost literally have stumbled over him. So both Commander and Chief Constable were right, according to their lights; the man was taken in before it was even known that he was missing, so the escape was over before it had officially started. This put the camp authorities in the right. On the other hand, he was collected outside the wire, which he had cut, so he was beyond the camp, therefore he had escaped, and this made the Chief Constable right.

Escape attempts usually had two things in common: they were insufficiently prepared; some of them seemed to be made on mere impulse. Even the trio who may have tunnelled their way out of Peveril failed to take so much as a sandwich with them; the three Dutchmen who escaped from Mooragh had no rations for the long sea journey they had set themselves. And in only one case in all the other escape efforts did a man have food rations with him.

The camp that gave the most trouble was inevitably Peveril. For much of the war it housed the men with hate in their veins. It also took the men who had got through the wire from Douglas or Mooragh and who might be expected to try again. In all twenty-three men escaped from Peel, apart from the three who tried unsuccessfully to get away by sea, and of that twenty-three only one was at liberty more than three days; most of the others were gathered up in less than two, sometimes after a mere hour or two.

The Peveril record shows one considerable achievement by the authorities. The break-out that led to the riot in September 1941 was followed by the arrival of the Metropolitan Police under Sam Ogden, who did not stay permanently on the island; he went back to Scotland Yard after a year. Yet for fifteen months after he took over control at Peveril not a single escape attempt is reported. He was undoubtedly a fine example of a senior policeman and administrator. While he was busy restoring order at Peveril, his son was reported missing in the first thousand-bomber raid, the attack on Cologne on 30 May 1942. Weeks later it was learned that the young man was not killed. He spent the rest of the war as a POW and then returned to the London police.

When the escapes did start again at Peveril, the next man out was a Jew of Czech origin whose behaviour and attitude suggest that he was nothing if not eccentric. The date was 6 December 1942. Peveril, like the other camps, had houses or groups of houses for different classes of inmate. In a complex camp a particular group became virtually a camp within a camp; in Peveril there was one unit made up of British Fascists, terrorists and the like, men detained under the Defence Regulations 18B; other groups contained the 12.5As, the alien detainees, including men who came from Occupied Europe whose loyalty and depend-ability had not yet been established; the P group were Germans.

The Czech Jew was an alien detainee: he was free for less than eleven hours before he was recaptured on the quay at Douglas. During his liberty he appears to have had a busy day. He blandly claimed that his escape had been a lark. He said that he had bet with the Metropolitan Police that he would get out, that he had obliged and had thumbed a lift to the Ramsey–Andreas area. Jurby and Andreas were near each other in the north of the island, both with RAF stations.

At Andreas, explained the wanderer cheerfully, he had had a talk with a Polish airman, had been inside the station and had left a challenging message on one of the aircraft. He said that the plane was fully fuelled and that he could have escaped if he had wanted to. But, of course, he never intended any such thing and had meant merely to absent himself for twenty-four hours as a protest. He was genial in his praise of the Camp Commander and claimed that his detention was entirely due to anti-Semitism in the Czech Air Force. He was said to be popular in the camp, even with the Nazis.

The most important remark in his interview was his assurance that any saboteur could get inside Andreas or Jurby. He caused a great deal of work, checking and cross-checking, involving the authorities, the Manx police and the RAF. His story was a strange rigmarole; it could have been true, partly true or so much rubbish. It was almost certainly nonsense, for there is no record that any of it was substantiated.

Although the Czech with the lively imagination was the first man to get out of Peveril main camp for more than a year, he was not the first Peveril man to make a bolt for freedom after the disturbances of September 1941. Ballaquane, the camp hospital, was situated at the north end of the main camp and still inside the perimeter wire. Two men there were found to be missing before breakfast on the morning of 30 August 1942, a Czech civilian air pilot of twenty-three, who was a patient, and a German of thirty-one, who was on the staff of the hospital.

The pilot was at liberty for less than six hours. He was found in the gorse at Rowany golf links at Port Erin—and was fast asleep. Rowany was on the fringe of the Port Erin internment area, and the search for the German was concentrated in that locality. The two men were known to be close friends.

More than a hundred special constables as well as the regular police spent a day and night combing the district. Their man was picked up the next morning in a curious manner. For some time there had been a regular work party leaving the married camp at 7.30 on weekday mornings, and it was automatically checked out at one of the control points. Its numbers were known. It was checked in again in the early evening, when the number had to tally with the morning record.

On this particular morning a quick-thinking special constable on the gate noticed that there was one more man in the shuffling column that he had been advised to expect. The German from Ballaquane Hospital was marching out as a member of the work party. It was a good ruse, but it failed. He was captured as he started to run for it. What he had been doing inside the camp is not on record.

The man who attempted to escape for what seems the obvious reason was in the minority. Men made the effort not with any hope of gaining permanent freedom but from a variety of simple impulses. A man wanted to draw attention to himself as a way of airing his grievances. He argued that if he could get out he would be caught and he could say his piece to the authorities. His case would be examined. To some escape was a challenge, the act of getting out being its own justification, even though it led nowhere; to get out, to prove that it could be done. It was something to scheme and work for; it broke the ceaseless monotony. Some men, incurable romantics, wanted to escape for the sheer thrill of it, with little thought of what would happen if and when they were outside. There were then the aimless ones, who would get out from hospital or away from a work party and in their confused state had nothing else to do but to walk back to the protection of the guards. They were the saddest group of all.

Precisely a month after the Czech's return to Peel, two more men duly escaped—but only for a day. One of them, on being searched, was found to have a dictionary, a New Testament and a book on Christian Science in his knapsack. He had provided for the soul but overlooked the needs of the body.

Seven Peveril detainees escaped from working parties or from hospital. The shortest time any of them was at liberty was twenty minutes. Some men escaped more than once; the two Irishmen who had been involved in the first break-out made a second attempt at the end of April 1943, having spent some time in prison in Liverpool between the two events. This time they had helped themselves to a sparking-plug, intending to fit it in the engine of an immobilized fishing-boat and get across to Ireland. They were picked up on the quay at Peel less than three hours later. At least they had shown serious intentions.

This certainly did not apply to a youngster at Peel a month earlier. This young man was British born of an Italian father. He was a working musician in dance bands and was aged twenty-two. He spoke English with a strong Cockney accent, having been born and brought up in London. He escaped from Peveril for less than seven hours, and on being brought back he explained that he had no particular reason for trying to escape— he just 'wanted a change of atmosphere'. His words. He topped this effort some time later, when again he escaped and this time just walked back to camp on his own.

There were many such in the camps, basically simple, bewildered men, without the slightest idea as to why they should be held in what they considered captivity. In reality, they stood no chance of escaping, and the more sensible of them knew this; some indeed said, on recapture, that they had known there was no way out. The fact was that the Manx were very much a closed society; it might not have been true that everybody knew everybody, but they all knew a great many. Servicemen in uniform would pass without drawing attention to themselves, but an internee who had broken camp or slipped away from a work party would be spotted at once. As a people the Manx had the farming community's ability to sniff out the hedgerows. The farmers and their families were the greatest aids to the police if an escape was reported.

It would be pointless to go through the list in detail; most items are repetitive in their naïvety. It can be said, though, that the most purposeful of all escapes concerned an Italian at Metropole who had had a visit from his wife and who knew that she was staying at a private hotel within a few yards of the camp. Accordingly he got out that night but was spotted at the hotel and the police were informed. He was recaptured in minutes, in the bedroom. He is alleged to have told the police that the English simply had no sympathy or understanding in these matters.

Of the camps in the centre of Douglas, Metropole was the only one recording any escape attempts. Hutchinson, Palace and Central were blameless. Apart from the man who was fond of his wife there were only two other attempts from Metropole, one by a man who had been a patient in the island's mental hospital on the other side of Douglas. He was a marine engineer seaman who spoke no English, and his escape consisted of walking back quietly across Douglas to the hospital. In the second attempt at Metropole two internees did get through the wire, but when they heard a guard approaching, they took refuge in the Crescent Hotel, which was next door. They were returned to camp after less than three hours, which had mostly been spent hiding in a bedroom. The date was 21 September 1942.

A man who had given serious thought to a successful escape break was a twenty-five-year-old special-class internee from Mooragh. He was in hospital with eye trouble when he escaped in February 1943. He spoke good English and he said later that he had a plan to join up with two others on the following day and fly to Europe. This would involve getting possession of a fuelled-up aircraft, and he was a pilot. How he proposed to steal a plane he never explained; nor did he explain why he was picked up at Foxdale the next day. He was found in one of the island's worked-out mining areas, walking away from the RAF stations which were fifteen or twenty miles to the north. His local geography was adrift. For guidance to Europe, however, he was found to have a nautical chart in his possession. This qualified him for six months' imprisonment in the island gaol in Douglas, after which he was transferred to the mainland.

Attempted escapes from hospitals were a nuisance to the police, as they all too often involved putting out a full alert, involving Home Guard and specials, but were themselves of trivial war risk. Too often the escapee was deranged. He might be violent until exhausted, but his chance of getting off the island or doing serious mischief was nil.

One such case was an Italian from Onchan, aged thirty-five, who was being taken by ambulance to the island's mental institution—Braddan Mental Hospital, usually known to the Manx as Ballamona. The date was 26 June 1942. Quite a lot happened before he arrived there, for the ambulance broke down. The escorting soldier jumped down to swing the starting-handle, so at once the internee pushed the interpreter aside and was down and off into the fields. The driver, the interpreter and the escort followed and attempted to overpower him, but he had armed himself with a stick into which he had notched a jagged piece of tin that he found on the ground. It took four policemen finally to seize and handcuff him, but not before he had sustained a wound on the forehead, for which the police courteously gave him first aid before driving him to Ballamona at the end of his interrupted journey. One question arises but the answer is simple. Why did the escorting soldier fail to shoot the man as he ran? Merely because he did indeed carry a rifle, but it would not have been loaded. Escorting soldiers did not have live ammunition issued for odd jobs of this sort.

The case, unimportant in itself, is interesting in that on 17 August, after he had been in hospital almost two months, the same man escaped from Ballamona, dressed in pyjamas and dressing-gown. Warning went out that he might be dangerous when challenged. He was at liberty until nearly midnight on the following day. Eventually he was found at Quarter Bridge, on the main cross-island road leading into Douglas. He was little more than a mile from the hospital, was utterly exhausted and made no protest at being taken back there.

Many of the 'escapes' from hospitals and from field work parties were that sort of nuisance. There were cases of men getting away from a working party and walking back to the camp they had come from; cases, too, of men sneaking out of hospital and going back 'home' to the barbed wire.

Escape attempts continued and even occasionally took place after the war in Europe had ended on 8 May 1945. Internees and detainees could not be pitchforked back into a world that was devastated. Authority had much to organize. The camps became smaller and smaller, until finally the remaining men were all concentrated into Peel, the last camp of them all, which closed with the repatriation back to a shattered Germany of the last German on the island, except for a limited number of POWs who stayed on for nearly seven months.

The attempted escape that could be regarded as the final one to be remotely serious occurred from Mooragh when two men were found to be missing at morning roll call on Monday 12 March 1945. They had in fact escaped at about 9.30 the previous evening. Mooragh was one of the only two remaining men's camps on the island by that time, with a mix of nearly 700 men of various nationalities. The pair who nearly got away were German; one had been in trouble before under another name and may or may not have been a German army officer before the war. He was a special-class internee, aged twenty-eight. The second man had been a plumber, was thirty-seven and an ordinary-class internee. The younger man seems to have been the dominant.

They did not escape by cutting through the wire; they had done their homework. They had noticed a point where the wires were simply looped round a boundary post and twisted together. This constituted a weakness. They had merely to untwist the wire and a break was established, a gap made. They could work their way out through it. It was an unpleasant and skin-tearing business, and one of them was badly cut. A blood trail showed the way they had made off. However, they had prepared themselves for whatever befell by taking a stock of food with them—which made them unique among would-be escapees. They had no money, they spoke to no one; while on the run they slept in the fields, made no attempt at a break-in and lived rough. There was a wide search, and the police knew that it was only a matter of time. It was, but many elderly Manx on remote farms were extremely glad when they heard that the men had surrendered. The weather was cold and wet and misty; the fugitives were beaten by the climate. Their food had run out; they had lived on turnips lifted from the fields. On the Monday morning, at 7.45, they walked into the post office at Bride and surrendered to the sub-postmistress. But they had broken a record; they had been at liberty for a week, the longest would-be escape on the island in the entire war. They had also caused a lot of trouble; three hundred people had taken part in the search for them on the Sunday.

When interrogated at Ramsey police station, both men complained that they had lately been refused repatriation. One said he had come from South Africa and wanted to be sent back there; he had had many requests refused. Repatriation took a long, long time, arrangements were hard to make and men had to await their turn. The younger man complained that he was pro-Nazi and he should be in a camp for Nazis, and not one where there were mixed feelings. He was depressed at being behind barbed wire and 'decided to enjoy some freedom'. Both agreed that they knew they could never get off the island.

It was a matter for the Camp Commander, who sent them on for a short term of imprisonment in the Isle of Man gaol at Douglas. It was arranged that on their release the older man would be sent to Peveril, while the younger would be shipped over to Walton Prison, Liverpool.

While inside in Douglas, the younger man, the self-styled German army officer, told the police that he had hidden in bushes inside Jurby RAF Station and had several times tried to start up aircraft. He had gone to Andreas and made similar attempts. He had a lively imagination. He was not above contradicting his own stories. He complained that he had found aircraft that were not immobilized and he could have started up any of them and flown away. He boasted that it was easy to get onto either airfield, and he claimed that he had written 'Next time watch better' on one of the planes he examined. It was all self-confident stuff.

On the morning of his release from Douglas Prison he was taken under escort to the harbour, where he went into a lavatory and slashed his left wrist. He was moved to Noble's Hospital where, on being undressed, he was found to have eleven razor blades in a pack, three more loose and nine others in a small safety-razor box. He also had a two-bladed pocket-knife. A letter in German to his parents was found in one of his boots saying that he was proposing to commit suicide.

The sergeant in charge of the man's escort reported that he had been assured when the man was handed over that a search had been made and the man was carrying nothing.

Thus ended the last escape attempt that appeared to have had any thinking behind it. A few weeks later the war in Europe was over.

One escape attempt does not appear in the records as such,

because it did not get beyond the clutches of the vigilant Metropolitan Police at Peel. All the same, it ended up in the courts, and it is in many ways one of the most interesting of all these cases. It concerned a young man of eighteen variously described as Dutch or an American. The likelihood is that he had been born in Paramaribo in Dutch Guiana, and he was a Dutch citizen despite a British- or American-sounding surname, which may have been false. He was living in Holland at the time of the German invasion and he escaped to Britain by getting down through Spain to Gibraltar. From late 1942 onwards he was involved in one scrape after another and appears to have been a crafty and indolent type. In November 1942 he was sentenced to one month's imprisonment in Wallington for breaking the curfew regulations without authority and for carrying no alien's permit. Shortly afterwards he was fined for stealing £11 from a wallet. Early in 1943 he spent a month in prison for travelling without a permit, followed by six months in Hull for failing to produce his registration certificate. He was then detained, and eventually he reached Peveril in Peel where he was involved in two court cases.

In the first of these he and another detainee from X Camp, Peel, were caught by the Metropolitan Police while trying to escape by climbing over the perimeter wire near the gate at the lower end of Walpole Road, opposite the stores area and the Creg Malin. It was just before eight o'clock in the evening on 16 November 1943.

The pair were taken across to the hotel, then the headquarters for the London police, where they were searched. The Dutchman was wearing blue sailor's trousers and a blue jersey. He had kept his personal papers and a Home Office petition, and he carried a parcel containing a sailor's round hat with the initials USS, and among other things a sailor's blouse with United States stars on the collar. With these additives and the clothes he was standing in, he could have passed as an American Navy rating. When further examined, he was found to have in his shoes a US Navy Pass and a US Navy Identity Card in the name of Flash Sylt.

The second man, another young Dutchman, was also searched. He too was wearing blue sailor's trousers and a high-necked blue sweater. He too carried a parcel with similar contents. In one of his shoes the police found a US Navy Pass. He made an effort to snatch this while he was being searched and only succeeded in tearing it into two pieces. He did not carry a US naval identity card.

The two passes and the identity card were neat and super-ficially convincing but they did not stand close examination. They were forged. One of the hand stamps was partly drawn and inked over, while the circular badge of the US Navy Department had been cut from a letterhead and superimposed. How they were forged and who forged them was never known for certain.

The young man from Dutch Guiana, who came from Holland via Gibraltar in the middle of war, came up in court charged with 'forging a certificate of identity calculated falsely to suggest that he, or some other person, was acting in the service of the Government of the USA' and also with having possession of a forged official pass.

He received three months' imprisonment for his ingenuity. His record later showed that in the autumn of 1944 he was given six months for larceny, based on several petty thefts from Peel Camp. He was a strange case; the war camps recorded not a few like him.

Most crime from the camps that came up into the courts amounted to precious little more than a series of examples of idle hands filling idle time with trivial enterprises. Exceptionally, some cases showed ingenuity.

The prize for the most practical crime surely went to an Italian who first came up in court charged with filing a few grains of silver from the edges of coins. This was a laborious way of making a fortune, and while in Onchan in February 1944 he built and operated an illicit still, not knowing that the distilling of duty-free liquor had been a well-established crime around the Irish Sea for many years, amounting to something of a popular pastime in some areas.

He may have been a welcome benefactor in Onchan, but he was transferred to Metropole by the time police enquiries were completed, and he came up in court at the end of September to be fined the startling amount of £200, which was the traditional and fixed penalty in Manx law for boiling up illicit hooch.

A crafty farmer might enjoy distilling and even selling his favourite tipple but he would be very careful not to be found out, if it meant so heavy a penalty. The prisoner, an internee with very little credit to his account, could never pay such a fine. The matter had eventually to be resolved by the Lieutenant Governor, who signed an edict reducing the fine to £10 in this special case.

22

Turn of the Soil

At least a year before the main repatriation of so many women internees in August 1944, the Isle of Man had become aware of a changing pattern to its life. The seaside landladies realized that a holiday season was at last developing, after so many lean years.

It was a real holiday rush, although but a miniature of the splendid days before the war when more than 700,000 visitors a year would cross to the island of seafood and escallonia. Once more there were reports of how upwards of a thousand people were left behind on the quayside at Fleetwood. By the first week in August people were spending two or even three nights in queues in the streets around the docks, and at the request of the Steam Packet Company the London Midland and Scottish Railway put up posters in its stations warning intending travellers of the difficulties of getting to the island. Servicemen and officials were priority passengers.

The busiest week-end followed what would normally have been the August bank holiday. People were stranded at both ends of the journey; returning holiday-makers could not get back, intending arrivals could not get across. VIPs, of course, had no difficulty. Herbert Morrison, the Home Secretary, made another of his frequent visits to the island, staying at Government House. He made it his business to visit various internment camps.

Another visitor from the headlines was Lady Maud Montgomery, mother of the General who was leading the Eighth Army in a sandstorm of victory. She took back with her a Manx kitten for herself and a Manx travelling-rug for her son.

November 1943 had produced a significant insight into the mind of the detainee and the more hardened internee. The Board of Agriculture's annual report stated that the number of male workers in the Manx farming industry had gone down from nearly 1,800 at the outbreak of war to 1,027 on 4 June 1943. So many men had been called up. Regular women workers had gone up from 93 to 167, a number of whom were Land Army volunteers. The report said, however, that internee and detainee labour could not always be relied on as strikes and passive resistance occurred at important seasons. To the pro-Nazi the harvest aided the British war effort and as such was *verboten*.

Relations between the Manx farmers and the internees were in the main very good indeed. The Italians were generally preferred to the Germans for they were considered willing and cheerful workers, whereas the Germans could be strictly correct. The normal routine had been for the men to be driven out under escort to the farms where they worked for the day. They took their midday meal with them, and every week the farmer paid the cost of their labour direct to the camp authorities. Men were not allowed to have real money, and it was an offence for it to be given or received, which does not mean that it did not change hands.

As the war developed, fewer guards were felt to be needed on the work parties. Sometimes the men were taken from camp to a bus stop and seen off on their journey. Some farmers, living in isolated areas, even arranged to drive up at a camp at eight every morning, collect their men and return them at five in the afternoon. They would be given petrol coupons to cover the journeys, the cost of the petrol to be paid by the farmer. It was a common sight to see cars from outlying farms waiting outside the front gate at some of the Douglas camps, with the farmer, frequently a woman, going into the guardroom and paying her dues once a week.

One woman, whose husband was a distinguished English lawyer, remembers how she collected her Italians from Central every morning and drove them north to Maughold. They were no trouble, and most of them spoke English. One had had a grocery business in Glasgow and spoke with a rich Scottish accent. Their first job had been to clear away gorse on some steep marginal land. For all such work the man received part of his earnings back from the camp in token money that he could spend inside the wire, and the rest went to his credit.

Years later, when so many of the Italians had been released back to civilian life in Britain, the Germans provided most of the available farm labour.

According to their performance, the men on the farms found themselves collecting that little bit extra that meant so much to an internee. Several picked up in escape attempts had British money on them. It had been given them by farmers in exchange for extra work. It was all against the rules but it went on. So was the feeding of the internees, who would arrive with two thick slices of bread and a piece of cheese and were at first not supposed to receive anything except a hot drink from the farm. However, it became commonplace for men to take their main daily meal alongside the local farm workers. Since soldiers from the camp carried out periodic checks, the internees would be given a meal to themselves in some barn or outhouse where they could be warned if trouble had arrived in the shape of a guard.

One farmer reported that he remembered the Germans as excellent workers but aloof men who brought no enthusiasm to their task. On the other hand, the Italians often had skills they were only too willing to use, especially if cash resulted. At least one Manx farmhouse had a mosaic of local chippings laid down on its kitchen floor by Italian craftsmen. In another case the Italians linked a fresh-water spring into a man-made reservoir and piped first-class water into a house that otherwise had none. It was for work like this that the hireling was worth rather more than his token money, and received it under the farm table.

The Douglas borough cemetery is situated almost directly opposite the grandstand that marks the start and finishing lines of the annual motor-cycle road races. Some years before the Second World War, the island's small Jewish community bought an area of what had once been a field there and made it the Jewish burial ground. Today it is one of the most concentrated reminders of wartime internment, for eighteen Jews are buried there, each grave neatly marked and maintained. The total of eighteen does not necessarily represent the full number of Jews who died in the island camps between 1940 and 1944, for it is noticeable that none of the dead came from Mooragh in Ramsey. They did, however, come from Peveril in Peel, from Onchan, from the women's camp across in Port Erin and from Central and Palace Camps in Douglas. Their recorded ages were significant and justified the early criticism that men were often interned indiscriminately in the great crisis of 1940 and that they could be well over sixty years of age.

The first Jew to die behind the wire was a man of forty-nine, who was buried in early September 1940, after dying in Hutchinson. Three more deaths followed before the year was out. A female infant died in the Camp Hospital at Port Erin on Armistice Day, 11 November, at the age of one day. Arthur Paunzen, the artist, died in Central on a 1940 date that appears to be unrecorded, and a man of sixty-three died in Oncham Camp on the last day but one of December.

The following year saw the death of an internee of seventy-nine. His age is on his tombstone, and his date of death is given as 4 April 1941. He was a German Jew from Onchan Camp, in normal life a book-keeper from Stoke Newington in North London. He died in the Falcon Cliff Hospital and had been suffering from hyper-tension.

There is a striking conflict of evidence about his age. The records of the Jewish burial ground unmistakably give him as seventy-nine at death. The official certificate gave the cause certified by a leading doctor in practice in Douglas; on record in the General Registry in Douglas it gives him as sixty, which, during the critical weeks of 1940, was considered the upward limit for internment. Extreme urgency sometimes explained the rules being broken.

The next man whose age was given as over seventy died one year later and was buried in April 1942. He too died in the Falcon Cliff Hospital, and he too had come from North London, where he had been described as a merchant. His age was given on his grave as seventy-three, the same as was entered in the Manx files. If there had been some sort of cover-up attempt on the age of the first man, there was none in the registration of the death of the second; seventy-three was indeed a remarkable age for an internee to die at after what was very obviously less than two years behind the barbed wire.

Three other Jewish internees, one of them a woman, were more than sixty years of age when they died in the island camps.

23

The Way Home

Ballaquane Hospital closed down in October 1944. Its modest buildings reopened within a few weeks with an intake of approximately sixty Finns from Mooragh. With the closure of the Peel Hospital, Giovanni Moneta was transferred back to Douglas as an orderly attached to the Falcon Cliff Hospital for internees.

There he was taken ill and had his appendix removed in Noble's Hospital. The surgeon was the Scot whose practice was on the front at Douglas and who had been the first of the Manx doctors to become attached to an internment camp when it all started back in 1940. The operation was subsequently significant to Maneta, for the successful appendectomy, although a routine matter in itself, was only the first favour he was to receive from the Scots doctor.

Meanwhile in their native land the Italians had gone through the very remarkable convolution of giving in to the Allies and shortly afterwards joining up with them in the war against Hitler.

This did not result in the immediate release of the remaining Italian internees on the Isle of Man, but the great steam-roller was crunching slowly across Europe, and although the end of the war was not yet in sight, victory was assured. It was therefore possible to offer war work to suitable internees who might not otherwise be offered it.

Moneta's chance came soon after he had been moved to Falcon Cliff and recovered from his operation. Men were wanted for war work in Liverpool at a factory manufacturing parachutes. He had no particular wish to leave the Isle of Man and still less to leave the occasional company of Margaret Cannell, but an opportunity to work in what was very nearly normality could not be missed.

So he went. This was a different life again. He was not yet free of all restrictions; he slept at the factory and ate in the canteen with the rest of the civilian workers, many of whom were women. He wore normal issue British battle dress, with a white circular patch on the back which alone revealed his status. Once, and only once, during his time in Liverpool did he see Margaret Cannell, although occasionally they had exchanged letters. It was her only visit to the mainland for the rest of the war.

He was free to roam about Liverpool in any way he wanted, and nobody gave him a second look. Life had reabsorbed him in the anonymity of the pavements.

Release came to Moneta in an unexpected way. After he had been working in Liverpool for only a few months, he had an industrial accident which left him with severe damage to a knee. By the time he recovered, the war was collapsing round the Nazi army; Europe was in a chaotic state. The thread for the parachutes was no longer needed at such desperate speed. The momentum of the munition factories was already starting to run down.

Moneta was advised that he needed a cartilage operation and that standing around heavy machinery was not for him in his condition. By now the war in Europe was over. He would be repatriated with the first of the Italian POWs to be sent back.

Weeks later he landed at Taranto, in the heel of Italy. There he stayed for a fortnight, until he received travel permits which took him home to distant Elba. He was luckier than some. But he had not finished with the Isle of Man. Far from it.

Later that year he invited Margaret Cannell to come to Italy and meet his parents. Months later the ex-internee and the nursing sister were married in Elba and spent their honeymoon in the hillside house of Giovanni's old shipmate Lanzardo Mattio, who had been with him at Metropole. Margaret Moneta's health was poor; she needed a more northern climate. Her husband applied to return and work in the Isle of Man. It was 1947, and a difficult time to seek permission. Then Moneta remembered the Scots doctor who had operated on him. He made the request; the papers were signed. He was free to return from one island to the other. It was the second favour he had received from the same doctor.

They came back to the Isle of Man and settled down in Douglas, where they had two children and now have six grandchildren.

All the internees who had put their names down for repatriation early in the war did not necessarily have to wait for the passing years, but almost all of them certainly did. Only a few went back to their homeland comparatively quickly. Disappointments were many and often bitter. The individual case had to be considered and compared with other applications. Exchanges had to be agreed: international arrangements had to be made and progressed through neutrals. It was a case that, where a substantial number wished to be called, only a relative few could be chosen.

The first repatriation had taken place back in the beginning of October 1941, when forty-three German women who had been interned in Port Erin since June of the previous year left the island to go down to Newhaven on the Sussex coast. There they joined two hospital ships which were to take badly wounded German prisoners of war back home under an exchange scheme. The routine for such an operation had to be organized by Sweden, and the journey to be routed through Gothenburg.

Those women were fortunate. It took three years all but a month for there to be another substantial repatriation, although steady efforts were made to secure one. There were always a great many obstacles; the approach to the enemy by the neutral power was a delicate business. In the camps rumour would lead to hope, then to mounting excitement and finally to disillusion and depression as it was reluctantly realized that one more camp dream had gone. Repatriation was not just the boat home for which the Nazi internee lived. The Italians who lived in London and Glasgow and even the non-Nazi Germans hoped fervently that those registered for repatriation would be lucky. For, in some mysterious way, a repatriation for the hard-liners meant that conditions were easing generally, and so they, the people left behind, would most likely be released back to the mainland and home the more quickly. Such was the impetuous logic of internment, and from time to time excitement went up and down like the temperature graph of a sick man. Bitter would be the disappointment. This particularly applied to the women's camp in Port Erin.

The next outgoing party after October 1941 was a small one, consisting of twenty-seven Japanese, who left Palace and Metropole Camps in Douglas for a northern port on the mainland. There they linked up with others of their countrymen, including diplomats, who were being repatriated under an agreement for the exchange of civilians. The Palace contingent was led by one Kano, who had been the manager in London of the Specie Bank of Yokohama and was known to camp guards, surely erroneously, as Viscount Kano. His men had attracted much quiet approval in Douglas. They were exceptionally lucky; having arrived in the Isle of Man in mid-December 1941, they were on their way home by a secret route early in the following July.

The largest single repatriation did not take place until 1 September 1944. Rather more than six hundred aliens—women, married couples and children—had opted to pull out from Port Erin, and at last, after so many setbacks, the turn of most of them had come. Their departure reduced the internee population of the small resort to fewer than four hundred. More than a hundred internees were also repatriated from the men's camps in the same party, bringing the total of detainees and internees remaining on the Isle of Man, men and women, to fewer than two thousand.

The *Mona's Herald* described the final scenes with a patriotic flourish. In the early hours of Friday morning, it wrote a little breathlessly, a special steamer glided out of the darkness of Douglas carrying six hundred aliens from Port Erin on the first stage of their journey to the darker life of their doomed German homeland. It was an accurate enough prophecy, although there was much fighting ahead across western Europe.

The internees from the men's camps had already boarded the Manx steamer. The contingent from the south arrived later by special train. It included 470 women and 25 children, some of whom had been born in the camp. They were taken to the quayside in relays by a small fleet of six buses.

Elaborate precautions, we are assured, were taken for the departure, and a large force of auxiliary police patrolled Douglas railway station. All busloads were escorted by London police-women stationed at the Port Erin camp. Police guarded the entrance gates, and about a hundred sightseers lined the railings on Station Hill to watch the women as they were driven off.

The repatriates looked just like a crowd of healthy holiday-makers, with the difference that they were not singing or joking; so said the *Mona's Herald*. Many carried Manx travelling-rugs as souvenirs of their four years on the island. It was not reported, but their luggage had been dumped at Port Erin's small railway station the previous day and carefully checked by the detachment of policewomen. These constables were experienced searchers who went through the work as a matter of routine, sometimes under rushed and difficult conditions. This time their task was heavy, but at least they had time for it. The Manx travelling-rugs reported by the local Press were only the outward and visible sign of the steady collecting that had been going on; the internees were proposing to return to Germany with tins of food, bought item by item from their modest earnings, with knitwear and with a substantial stock of sanitary towels. These last they had saved carefully from any surplus to requirements in their personal monthly issue, which was free and decidedly liberal as almost all of them had been on camp welfare. Allied intelligence was insisting that there was an acute shortage of such items in Germany, and luggage so liberally stocked would make good propaganda. The women themselves were willing collaborators on this one point: the small detachment of policewomen who had to buy theirs in the ordinary way took a jaundiced view as they checked the luggage and started to confiscate these items. Word quickly came down from the camp authority; the women were perfectly in order in taking as many as they could pack and were not to be discouraged. It made good sense to let them take them back to Germany. So take them back they did, sometimes even as the stuffing for soft toys.

The last of the women were aboard the *Rushen Castle* by ten o'clock on the Thursday night. They mostly walked briskly up the gangplanks, excited and happy; one was heavily pregnant. It did not look as if they were sorry to be leaving. They sailed soon after midnight and, after a very rough crossing, reached Liverpool at breakfast time on the Friday morning. The *Drottningholm*, which housed an entirely different problem that was a police matter, had not been allowed to berth but was anchored in midstream. The internees were taken across to it by tender, but for reasons that had nothing to do with the repatriates it was some hours before the ship could set off. The party then sailed for Gothenburg, where they were exchanged for returning British prisoners of war and internees.

M. E. Mundy, special correspondent of the London *Daily Telegraph*, talked with the repatriates when they reached Sweden, about to start on the last leg of their journey home. Baron Kettleholdt, a former German camp leader, would not be quoted for publication. Herd Hanwerck, another leader, was very frank. When asked about their treatment, he replied: 'Food and billets were quite satisfactory, especially during the last two years in the married camp. Before that in the military camps conditions were not so comfortable, but have since improved.

'We have no complaints and all of us are grateful for many considerations and the fair treatment we received from Commander Cuthbert, the British chief of the Isle of Man camps.'

C. R. M. Cuthbert was, of course, commandant of the women's and married camps at Port Erin. He was not in charge of the men's camps and never had been.

24

The Final Party

As the months passed after D-Day, the enemy slowly yielded ground under the impact of the massive assault. More and more German prisoners of war were being taken. The Isle of Man had to be prepared for new arrivals, who would come pouring in to surrender ever more eagerly as their resistance cracked. Arranging for such huge movements of men was a business that could be anticipated and planned for by the War Office in London and by similar institutions in other Allied countries. War and the prisoners thereof were their business. The men in the WO had plenty of precedent for this type of operation and could handle it with scarcely a hitch, unlike the difficulties in the early months of the war during the round-up and temporary internment of thousands of mostly innocent refugees from the Hitler terror.

On D-Day the only camps still operating on the island, apart from Port Erin, were Mooragh, Metropole, Peveril and Onchan. Hutchinson had closed in March. Its 228 inmates were moved over to Peel.

The military soon started the business of cleaning up the empty square and preparing it for future occupants. The work was not completed until November, when reporters were invited to inspect what had been an internment camp. Everything was said to be in good condition; not one of the locked cupboards left by the landlords when they originally departed had been broken into, they said. Hutchinson had a good record. Its first internees had taken pride in keeping the central garden in good trim. The square was the quad. Learning went on around it.

Much had been done to the houses by the camp authorities, including the installation of shower-bath units and dressing-cubicles, a modern laundry complex and a workshop, where once there was even a substantial business making siren suits from Manx cloth. There was also a modest auditorium with a stage and dressing-rooms, which had also served as a lecture hall for the camp's 'university'.

Metropole was the next to be closed. It had 482 men at the start of October 1944 and had been cleared out by the first week of November. Local newspaper representatives were shown around it within a matter of weeks. They reported favourably, saying that there had been no time for renovation or decoration and that the private hotels of which the camp was mostly made up showed signs of wear and tear 'but not to an excessive degree'. Structural damage to the fabric was comparatively small.

Rumours soon went round the island that up to 7,000 German prisoners of war were likely arrivals, providing the Manx with more re-shuffling of furniture and effects. While householders had been obliged to leave basic furniture for internees, the War Office now insisted on providing its own equipment for POWs. This meant that a great mass of chattels had to be cleared out from the houses involved and steadily transferred to Derby Castle, which was being used as a huge depository.

This was yet another job for the guard troops. The furniture, having been commandeered in the name of the Lieutenant Governor years earlier in the war, was now the property of the Manx Government, who put a Londoner, H. Burtenshaw, in charge of the operation of sorting, identifying, repairing, storing and stacking thousands upon thousands of individual items. Burtenshaw had spent his previous three years as a government valuer of blitzed property in England, after which he had retired to the island. He now went to work again. The Derby Castle Variety Theatre, where internees had once assembled to meet their womenfolk from Port Erin, was soon packed to capacity with all the basics of boarding-house furniture. There were more than 2,000 chairs stacked in one area; the stage was piled with kitchen tables, dressers and what one imaginative observer described as a silent chorus of wardrobes.

Records were made of every item and of the house from which

it came. Cleaning and repairs were then started. It was a formidable job, taking many people many months of hard work. Never before had there been such an undertaking in the Isle of Man. Cabinet-makers, joiners, polishers—all the trades were busy for months after the war was over.

At the end of 1944 there were only 318 men and women left in the two camps over in the west of the island, and 1,011 men divided between Mooragh and Peel. Ballaquane was closed once more as no longer necessary. Onchan Camp had been cleared in November, to be made ready for prisoners of war. The old Douglas camps were now military establishments or POW cages.

In the first week of 1945 the island saw the last of the men from the Metropolitan Police, who had been in charge of Peveril since the trouble in October 1941. They returned to duty in the London area, and in the last year of its life the detainee camp was controlled entirely by the military.

Many of the London contingent had brought their wives and families with them during their service, and it was quite a large party that went off on the morning boat. In a few cases the families stayed behind on the island, their homes in London having been destroyed in the air raids. Praising them warmly, the Manx Press insisted that the Londoners had always given their time generously to help local efforts for Manx and national charities.

Month by month the POW population of the island rose steadily, and the internee figures dropped. The war in Europe finished on 8 May 1945, and by then there were only 1,198 left, including 664 men at Mooragh and 278 internees made up of women and married couples, at Port Erin. Then on 25 May another 295 internees left the island for Fleetwood. They were the last shipment but one and were mainly men from Mooragh and Peveril. By now the women's and married camps were almost empty, with no more than 200 left where there had once been nearly 4,000.

Mooragh closed on 2 August 1945, leaving behind only 472 men detained in the various sections of Peveril.

The final party went away on 5 September 1945, when a Steam Packet ship took 580 aliens to Fleetwood, 180 coming from Port Erin and 400 from Peel. Almost all of them were Germans. They included Dr Hermann Scholz, who had spent five years as an internee. A special train took them from Fleetwood to London, where they were taken on to a dispersal camp at Stanmore, near Harrow.

The party from the mixed camps at Port Erin included sixty women and twenty-seven children, eleven of whom had been born on the island. There was one baby, only a few months old, who was brought to the pier with its mother in a car driven by one of the Home Office female staff. Two stretcher cases also arrived from Port Erin, brought to the ship by ambulance; one was a German suffering from spinal trouble, the second a Japanese with rheumatoid arthritis. A third case was driven up from Noble's Hospital having recently undergone an operation for a duodenal ulcer. There were a number of other sick cases of a less serious nature, looked after by orderlies of the Royal Army Medical Corps.

The men from Peel were marched from Douglas Station to the King Edward Pier, each man carrying his hand-luggage. The heavier belongings were brought to the pier by lorry. It was like the original arrival at the pierhead at Ramsey all that time ago, but in reverse.

One elderly alien dropped his case as he was boarding the steamer; food rolled and fell seawards. He was carrying more than a dozen eggs, a pat of butter and two bottles of milk. He was indeed leaving the island of milk and honey.

Some of the clothing worn by the aliens had been manufactured from local wool, woven on home-made looms, and some of the suits they wore had been reasonably tailored inside the camps.

Inspector W. H. Howard of the Metropolitan Police was in charge, and there was an armed guard of about fifty members of the Pioneer Corps.

The party was over. The road back to Germany was to be both sad and sour. From London the men were taken on to Ostend under military guard. They were totally unprepared for what they found. It was a new, different and horrifying world. Dr Scholz, now still practising in Berlin, reminded the writer that he had been collected as an enemy alien in London early in the war and had reached the Isle of Man after a stay in various mainland camps ending with Huyton. Until it was over, most of the men had seen little of the bombings. Now, on the return journey, they

had passed some of the damaged areas in London and seen more
again going through Belgium. But crossing into Germany they
found themselves in a devastated land in which life survived in a
shattered, skeleton-like form. One party was taken on to
Munster, where the military guard turned and left them. They
were alone, strangers, but back home, where it seemed that there
was no home; only one vast clearing-up operation. It was weeks,
said the doctor, before he went to his native Berlin, only to find
that, apart from the military presence, there was scarcely any city
left. They had come to this from the Isle of Man, where the farmer
made his own butter and a worker was well fed. Dejected,
puzzled and a little afraid, they had seen their guards leaving
them without word or signal of goodbye as they disappeared
back to the safety and sufficiency of the British Army of Occupa-
tion, with the men from the distant island now left to the bleak
hospitality of a roofless Munster.

These men, standing bewildered in the rubble of a shattered
city, were at the final passing-out parade of an army whose
muster on the Isle of Man had started six years earlier. Its ranks
had held hearly 14,000 men and women at its peak, most of them
united in their opposition to Germany and all united in their
temporary incarceration by the British. Now its remnants at last
disbanded, months after the war was over. No army, surely, had
ever known such a proportion of talent; any list of the rank and
file of the men interned, mostly for short duration, would be
littered with names that became internationally distinguished in
science, in the arts, in academic life and in the boardrooms of
commerce. Taken almost at random, the higher administration
was represented by Sir Claus Moser, statistician, man of many
talents, patron of the arts and Chairman of the Royal Opera
House; there were many academics including men such as Sir
Nikolaus Pevsner and Professor Geoffrey Elton; scores of
internees left the camp to return to the universities and to
scientific research; Professor Paul Polani, the geneticist, became
one of the senior surgeons and consultants; Lord Weidenfeld was
to join the publishers; men who were to become directors of
important companies included Ronald Grierson of General
Electric and Sir Alex Alexander, later chairman of Lyons; men
destined to become the dominant figures in vast business enterprises included Sir Charles Forte, who founded an international
catering enterprise, and R. W. 'Tiny' Rowland, head of the vast

Lonrho conglomerate, who joined his family on the island as a youth; there were authors, journalists and even a distinguished chess analyst; there were instrumentalists who enriched the leading orchestras, and individual musicians who teamed up to become respected groups wherever music was taken seriously; there was del Giudice, the film producer whose work went round the world, and Mario Zampi, the sardonic film director whose sense of humour later made him famous; and there were the artists at table, the owners and cooks behind some of the best restaurants in Britain. They were but some of the roll of celebrities of the future. The rest were mainly modest folk, who had been released back to the war production line or the kitchen sink, and some volunteers to the Army. So let the obscure remain in what is left of their anonymity.

Index